The Laws of the Game

This book applies theories, methods, and concepts from game studies to soccer. This is a game studies book about soccer that studies the rules and design of soccer and the impact that technology has on the game's evolution.

The book comprises nine chapters that approach soccer from different game studies angles. The different chapters study the game off the pitch (the design), on the pitch (the gameplay), and around the pitch (the culture). The book establishes conversations with game studies, illuminating what we take for granted in the field and showing what is left to study. At the same time, it provides readers with a deep understanding of the importance of soccer, why we should pay attention to it, and how it reflects broader trends in culture, technology, politics, and play.

This book will be of great interest to game, media, and sports scholars, as well as undergraduate and graduate students in those fields.

Miguel Sicart is Professor at the IT University of Copenhagen, where he is currently the Head of the Center for Digital Play.

Bo Kampmann Walther is Associate Professor at the Department of Design, Media, and Educational Science, University of Southern Denmark, Denmark.

The Laws of the Game

A Game Studies Book about Soccer

Miguel Sicart and Bo Kampmann Walther

CRC Press
Taylor & Francis Group
Boca Raton London New York

CRC Press is an imprint of the
Taylor & Francis Group, an **informa** business

Designed cover image: Shutterstock

First edition published 2026
by CRC Press
2385 NW Executive Center Drive, Suite 320, Boca Raton FL 33431

and by CRC Press
4 Park Square, Milton Park, Abingdon, Oxon, OX14 4RN

CRC Press is an imprint of Taylor & Francis Group, LLC

ISBN: 9781041068037 (hbk)
ISBN: 9781041067184 (pbk)
ISBN: 9781003636762 (ebk)

DOI: 10.1201/9781003636762

Typeset in Minion
by Newgen Publishing UK

Contents

Acknowledgments

Miguel

Ever since we wrote the contract to publish this book, I've considered my career to be fulfilled. I have been a games scholar for over two decades and finally wrote about the game I love the most. So first of all, thanks to my co-author Bo, who helped make writing this book a process as pleasing as watching FC Barcelona take the ball and pass the ball.

A heartfelt thank you to my colleagues at the Center for Digital Play—IT University of Copenhagen for patiently enduring all my conversations that ended with football analogies. Additionally, I sincerely thank Óliver Pérez Latorre and his colleagues at the MEDIUM research group, Universitat Pompeu Fabra in Barcelona. I completed this book while on sabbatical there, and the time and space I was given to work on my chapters made a massive difference in the quality of the text.

Talking about my sabbatical in Barcelona from 2024 to 2025: thank you to Atlètic Poblenou and the 2011 Infantiles team for a year of enjoyable games. And thanks to 2024–2025 Hansi Flick's FC Barcelona for reigniting a style of play that brings joy. It was a privilege to witness its flourish live at the Estadi Olímpic Lluís Companys.

I have read nearly as much about football as I have watched games. But I've learned the game's true meaning mostly on the sidelines and through my engagement with a local Danish club. This book wouldn't exist without B1908's team of kids born in 2011, where my youngest son plays. My insights into the game, why it matters, and how it does are a result of many hours spent with other parent coaches like Heidi Colding, Ian McKenzie, Thomas Løtzsch, Kenneth Kræmmer Mortensen, Troels Riis Poulsen, and Thomas Christensen. This book is also dedicated to Silas and his teammates in B1908.

Finally, I want to give a very special thanks to my friend and fellow *culé* Niels Pedersen, whom I met thanks to Sergi Roberto's winning goal against Paris Saint-Germain on March 8, 2017, which was the best possible start to a beautiful friendship.

While the excitement of elite football is captivating, the real game occurs every day by people everywhere. Wherever you see someone kicking a ball, there's a Champions League final in the making. This book is dedicated to my dad, who taught me how to watch the game, and to those who play football, anywhere and everywhere.

Bo

You know what? Just copy and paste Miguel's first paragraph above and replace "Barcelona" with "Real Madrid". Muhaha!

In my childhood in the 1970s, I had heroes like the Dutch Johan Cruyff, the Brazilian Éder Aleixo de Assis, the German Paul Breitner, and, of course, the "flying" Dane, Henning Jensen, who joined my team, Real Madrid, in 1976 and stayed for three seasons. Thanks to my dad, who passed away in early 2024, for ensuring my football lens was both wide and detailed.

Around the 2006 World Cup, I joined the Danish newspaper *Dagbladet Information*, writing long-form journalism about international football. It's been 20 years and counting, and—among many others—I wish to thank Rune Lykkeberg, Jon Faber, Jon Jørgensen, and the late, brilliant Lasse Ellegaard.

A big thanks to Jakob Genz for being a decade-long friend, a stubborn Chelsea fan, and a football-book collaborator. And above all, to my family—Anne, Jonathan, and Semina—for graciously and lovingly learning to live with someone shaped by the rituals and seasons of football.

Introduction

Why does anyone love football? It's a game that requires us to use our feet to control and pass a hard, bouncy ball, trying to shoot it into a goal that feels both too big and too small at the same time. The goals are placed at opposite ends of the field, which is so long that sprinting back and forth more than a few times becomes exhausting. The game can last over two hours when played by the official rules. These rules make football a complex sport, with offside and handball regulations that challenge players' sense of fairness and test spectators' patience. It's also an unusual sport, with few goals scored and a category of players—midfielders—whose role is crucial for keeping the game flowing, and confusing to those who aren't interested in the sport. Midfielders don't score or block goals; they stay in the middle of that long field, occupy space, and pass the ball. The rules don't strictly define their role, yet playing without them is impossible.[1] Football is a strange game, yet it's the most popular sport on Earth. The joy of football comes from this very strangeness—a sport that shows how complex, creative, and imaginative we can be as people.

This book aims to provide a new perspective on understanding the game. We, the authors, are scholars of games. Our academic careers have centered on studying games, especially digital ones: how they work, their cultural

DOI: 10.1201/9781003636762-1

roles, how people create them, and why. We have been part of the field of game studies, which has developed a vocabulary for understanding games as cultural, technological, and social expressions. We both love games, but we love no game more than football. That's why we wrote a game studies book focused on football.

The book you're reading now is an introduction to how to think about football using ideas from game studies. A few decades of studying games have given us some concepts and terms that are very helpful in explaining why football, that incredible game, is so popular. Throughout the book, we will use ideas like possibility space or metagaming to explain why games are so engaging, how the midfield works, or why football is 11 versus 11 and Germany always wins. This book will give you some new words to describe football, different ways to look at the game, and maybe even ways to play it.

We are not pundits or former players. Our authority doesn't come from hours on the pitch, professional experience, or watching Canadian third-division games on YouTube. We are game scholars, so our authority comes from the privilege of having spent our careers thinking about and teaching about games of all kinds. Our authority comes from being outsiders to the world of football.

But don't be confused by our use of "authority". We don't seek to explain why football matters or how you should think about it. Ultimately, this book is a love letter to football. We want to share the words and ideas that help us express how watching and playing football makes us feel. This is a book that offers new ways of describing the joys, sorrows, worries, and comforts of football.

Because if there is one idea we want to communicate with this book, it is that we love football because it unites us. Why does anyone love football? Because it's something we pass down. Anyone who loves the game has at some point kicked a ball and discovered that it's incredibly fun to try to do with your feet what's so easy to do with your hands. And then, when that basic joy is found, someone else joins you and encourages you to do it together. We love football because it brings us together. We become fans of a club, take on a specific role as players, join a league, and, through all these things, share that fundamental joy of togetherness.

Football is also a sport that brings generations together. Someone might tell you why and how you support your team, how it's something passed down, part of the family, an irrational and unexplainable tribal attachment to a shirt and colors that somehow brings comfort when loneliness hits and joy when we celebrate together. The love for football is hereditary and shared like all sports—a universal language anyone can understand. It allows people to travel around the world and find like-minded fans. Football can be the perfect way to show what our societies could be: open, supportive, without borders, without excluding labels, connected by the thrill of competition and a feeling of joy.

But football is also a dangerous game. Modern sports are driven by economic and political interests that seek to commercialize, manipulate, and politicize our enjoyment. Despots form teams and buy their way into history or take control of tournaments because they know football makes people happy and want to exploit that happiness for their own gain. This book also acts as a warning, aiming to show that the love of the game is, like all great loves, complex and can be turned against us or, worse, used to foster hatred toward others.

But we remain hopeful. If we better understand the game and explain why we love it, we'll see that there is no place in football for hate and the exploitative economics that have taken over. We can admire the stars, appreciate the tactical innovations, and cherish match day when, along with 6000 or 60000 others, we laugh and cry together. If we can describe our love for the game, it might be harder for that love to be taken away from us. That is, ultimately, why we wrote this book.

This book originates from a conversation between friends who share a common interest in football from different perspectives. Bo writes about football for a major Danish newspaper, explaining to a broad audience the importance of the game's history and phenomenology. Bo's view blends a solid understanding of the past with a future-oriented outlook and regards the game as a playful performance. Miguel, a more traditional academic, has mainly published journal articles and book chapters on rules and the relationship between football and its digital simulations. His approach to football also stems from coaching a kids' side. The hours spent on the pitch trying to teach children to play together are only matched with the hours spent reviewing all relevant research and literature on youth training.

But most importantly, Bo is a Real Madrid fan, and Miguel is an FC Barcelona fan. Fortunately, the rivalry between our clubs did not translate into a rivalry in our writing, and we managed to complete this book without major disagreements. However, we have subconsciously drawn from our rivalry in writing this book, as there is a constant back-and-forth, or as it is called in Spanish, a *tuya-mía*,[2] in our arguments. This book shifts between focusing on the historical roots and formal principles of the game and embracing the freedom of playing as the game evolves toward its data-driven future. We have written about the history of the sport, but we have also examined how computational technologies, digital media, and the data revolution are transforming our understanding of football. We have analyzed tactics and the structure of the game, but we have also tried to explore what makes a player unique and the role creativity plays in the game. Additionally, we have looked at the cultural aspects of football—how it can reflect history and tradition while also mirroring the development of platform capitalism.

A common theme in football writing describes the rivalry between FC Barcelona and Real Madrid as a tension between two schools of thought that need each other to succeed, despite their differences. Real Madrid has a winning culture, while FC Barcelona is known for its philosophy of how the game should be played. Similarly, this book focuses on different schools of thought that offer various interpretations of football. It should be read as a *tuya-mía*—a game where one person catches an idea, plays with it, and passes it to the other who is in a better position to advance toward our goal. This book is also a one-two with the reader: we want you to choose whichever ideas you find compelling and use them to watch the game, especially to discuss it with others. Football is a game of exchanges: passing the ball and receiving the ball. Enjoying football should also be a game of exchanges, with ideas, pleasures, pains, victories, and defeats flowing back and forth.

Our goal with this book was to apply the vocabulary of game studies to the game of football. After all, since the late 1990s, game studies has been developing concepts that help us understand how games are made, experienced, consumed, and communicated. It seemed obvious to us, as professional game scholars, to examine the world's most popular sport through the lens of our discipline. Therefore, this book introduces concepts related to game studies, such as possibility space and debates about rule aesthetics, to how we analyze football. At the same time, the book aims to legitimize the study of sports as a part of this academic field. It is rather odd that sports have been a marginal topic in game studies. How can we study games if we don't consider sports as essential examples in this conversation?

Our answer is this book: an invitation to see sports as part of a broader family of technologies designed for play we conventionally call "games".

We could write more about the book—what it includes and why we organized it as we did. But we want to finish this introduction by returning to the idea of football as something shared. Both of us have a history with the game. We have learned to watch it, with our preferences shaped by the people who taught us what to look for and what to admire. Football is a game that is trained and communicated; it's a bond that connects us through an idea of what the game represents and with the people who share that idea. How you are taught to appreciate football shapes how you think of it and why you may love it. With this book, we want to give readers a new lens to view the game—a new perspective and a new vocabulary for the game.

This vocabulary, inherited and adapted from game studies, is our way of giving readers more methods to express why they find something interesting. This is not a book about the ultimate knowledge ever possible to be developed about football. It is a book about love for the game. And love needs words. With this book, we want to offer just another way of expressing what we feel when we see Messi, or the English Women's National team, or that moment when Emiliano Martínez made an impossible save in the dying moments of extra time of a World Cup final, securing Argentina's third title in the winter heat of Qatar.

We also want this vocabulary to go beyond that mediated football. We want these words to also describe the feeling that happens when a group of strangers gather around a pitch on a summer day and manages to score a goal after a series of clever passes. We want to capture the joy of watching a team of young kids stop chasing the ball and start moving as a team. We aim to give words to the pagan pilgrimages to stadiums and to the vibrant, fleeting friendships that form with strangers when watching any game together.

Football can be an ugly game that exposes people's worst sides. Maybe the top level of the sport, the elite stage, is being overshadowed by content platforms and sportswashing efforts. But this sport remains so popular because it fundamentally belongs to us—those who play, watch, and enjoy it. Football's reach starts on the pitch but extends worldwide, which is probably the game's core principle: how the laws of the game bind us together.

NOTES

1 As we will explain later on in this book, this statement is only true for football *after* the establishment of the offside rule. To a large extent, the offside rule invented not only the modern game, but also the roles of players and their positions.

2 In Spanish, that expression means "yours and mine", or better, "yours, then mine", and it is used to explain the fundamentals of the distinctive style of playing football based on the rapid association among players using short, quick passes coupled with movement. Spanish journalist Andrés Montes made globally popular the expression "tiki-taka", which is synonym to *tuya-mía*.

CHAPTER 1

The Universal Game Around the World

WE ABSOLUTELY ADORE FOOTBALL. In that sense, we are stupid taxi drivers. You will have to read to the end of the chapter to learn why. We call it *football*, and not soccer, like the Americans. We are European, stupid taxi drivers.

In this opening chapter, we map the dynamic relationship between universal rules and national differences in football and introduce the idea of a *possibility space*, the domain of options created by rules and explored through tactics. We will pay more attention to this concept later in the book. We will spread it out and, most of all, discuss it through the lens of game studies. In this chapter, we look historically at how key laws (notably offside) shape creativity. We show how national cultures inflect style, keeping an eye on Argentina, the Netherlands, Brazil, Italy, and others. And we discuss the tension between structure and freedom that makes football both a global language and a deeply local art.

For proof it's always been gloriously messy, return with us to 1872. That year, one of the first international football matches took place between England and Scotland at the West of Scotland Cricket Club's ground in Partick, Glasgow. Politically, the relationship between the two nations was influenced by the ongoing effects of the Acts of Union (1707), which had merged England and Scotland into a single kingdom, though distinct

DOI: 10.1201/9781003636762-2

national identities remained. The match was a milestone, not just because of the outcome—a 0-0 draw—but because of the uncertainty it reflected about football's future. The rules were still evolving, teams had not yet mastered the game's nuances, and debates about what football should be were widespread (some things never change). During this inaugural game, the English and Scots struggled to understand each other's playing styles as well as the official rules, which were still in the process of becoming standardized. Even something as basic as the offside rule was being tested in real time.

Following their version of the laws, the English team believed that a player was offside if they were positioned ahead of the ball. At the same time, the Scots, influenced by their own regional interpretation of the rules, seemed to place less emphasis on this restriction. As a result, while undeniably thrilling, the game itself was chaotic. Players would rush forward with abandon, leaving little room for strategic control. It was a far cry from the football we recognize today, with its well-defined laws and tactical precision.

Football is often heralded as the world's game. No other sport enjoys the same level of global participation in active play and spectator engagement. The FIFA World Cup and the Champions League are global broadcast successes, the results reaching the farthest corners of the planet. Yet despite its universal appeal, football is not a homogeneous experience. It is a game deeply embedded in the national cultures and histories of the regions in which it is played. How football is understood, experienced, and even named varies across continents, revealing critical intersections between culture and history. This rich complexity brings to the surface fundamental tensions between the playful freedom of the game and its more structured, rule-bound nature. This tension is not only visible in the ways football is played but also in the ways it is conceptualized and cherished.

Game studies provides us with specific words to study this back and forth between order and freedom. Like many other sports and games, playing football simultaneously straddles the worlds of *paidia* (playfulness, creativity, and spontaneity) and *ludus* (structure, rules, and competition).[1]

Etymologically, *paidia* (*παιδιά*) derives from Greek *pais* (*παις*), which means "child", as it names the open-ended frolic of play: improvisation, make-believe, exuberance without preset goals. *Ludus*, by contrast, is Latin and stubbornly polysemic: it means play, game, pastime, but also school, drill, training, even staged contest. That doubleness matters: ludus already fuses pleasure with discipline and competition with pedagogy, which is why "ludic" today can mean both playful and rule-governed. In the 20th century, Johan Huizinga's *Homo Ludens* (1938) framed play as a culturally constitutive, rule-bounded "magic circle". Roger Caillois (1958) sharpened the vocabulary, placing paidia and ludus at opposite poles of a continuum, and crossing that axis with his famous quartet of the types of game we play. *Agon* games take place within a field of fighting and competition.[2] *Alea* is all about chance and luck, like Russian roulette. *Mimicry* is the theatrical element in games, for instance, the joy of copycatting a role or a character you'd like to be. And finally, *ilinx* are games that make you dizzy, like roller coasters or circus stunts. From Gonzalo Frasca's early 2000s essays to Salen and Zimmerman's *Rules of Play* (2003) and Jesper Juul's *Half-Real*, from 2005, contemporary game studies adopted this dyad to describe how games oscillate between something out of control and something controllable.

Football is purpose-built for this oscillation: street potrero or beach kick-abouts (paidia) sediment into academy drills, tactical periodization, and law-bound competition (ludus). And then, 90 minutes at a time, ludus and paidia collapse into each other on a 105 × 68-meter stage, when the game is played.

This balance between paidia and ludus forms the heart of football's most compelling qualities. On the one hand, football is built on a formalized rulebook that defines the boundaries within which the game is played: offside, fouls, and match durations provide structure. On the other hand, the game also fosters moments of joyfully unexpected improvisation, where the beauty of a single player's creativity can break through the rigid framework and elevate the sport into something more than just a contest of rules. Perhaps even become art. Indeed, the Argentinians think so, as we shall see later. The game's possibility space, the ever-expanding horizon of what is imaginable and playable within the confines of football's formal structure, becomes a dynamic intermediary between these two forces. It represents the space between the rules and the strategies, where individual brilliance and team tactics can unfold in infinite variations.

OFFSIDE

The offside rule is one of the most fascinating examples of this interplay between structure and creativity in football. This rule is perhaps the most beautiful of them all, and certainly the most effective, as we will demonstrate in Chapter 3.[3] Often perceived as one of the more complex and debated aspects of the game, the offside rule is paradigmatic within the discussion of possibility space. It is a rule that imposes clear boundaries on the game, dictating where players can and cannot position themselves on the field. However, it is also a rule that offers endless tactical opportunities for innovation.

The key moment in establishing the modern offside rule came in 1925, but this was the result of a long history of changes. The concept of the offside rule dates to the beginnings of football and even earlier forms of football-like games. In the mid-19th century, when various forms of football were being played in schools and communities, the rules varied widely. The Cambridge Rules, first established 1848, included a primitive offside rule, where players were offside if they were ahead of the ball when it was played. This was a precursor to the modern offside law. However, when the Football Association (FA) was founded in England in 1863, and the first formal laws of the game were codified, the offside rule was outlined as part of the laws of the game. It was stricter than today's version. A player was offside if they were positioned ahead of the ball, with little consideration for the number of defenders or players between them and the goal. The rule was essentially designed to prevent goal-hanging, where players would wait near the opponent's goal for easy opportunities to score.

By the early 1920s, there was growing dissatisfaction with the way the offside rule was affecting the game: it had become too easy for defenders to stifle attacking play by crowding the goal area and forcing forwards to be offside. The offside rule at the time required a player to have at least three players (including the goalkeeper) between them and the goal to be onside. This meant that attackers often found it difficult to break through the defense, and games became increasingly defensive, with low-scoring matches. This created a wall of defenders around the goal, and attacking play suffered.

Then came the solution. In 1925, the International Football Association Board (IFAB) decided to reform the offside rule to encourage more attacking play. The key change was to reduce the number of players required to be between the attacking player and the goal from three to two. An attacker could be onside with just the goalkeeper and one other defender between them and the goal. It also meant more scoring opportunities. With fewer defenders required to keep a player offside, forwards had more opportunities to receive the ball in attacking positions. This led to more goals and a more exciting spectacle for spectators. It sparked the evolution of tactics, as the change forced teams to rethink their defensive strategies. Defenders could no longer rely solely on crowding the goal area and playing for offside traps. Instead, they had to focus on positioning and timing to avoid leaving attackers unmarked.

The offside rule is central to understanding how football, as a global phenomenon, reflects both standardization and local interpretation. In nations where a more direct and physical style is favored, such as in England or Italy, the offside rule often becomes a tool for tactical control and defensive dominance. In countries like Argentina or the Netherlands, where individual flair and tactical fluidity are more prevalent, the offside rule invites more creative and expressive approaches.

THE ARGENTINIAN AND THE DUTCH GAME

In Argentina, football reflects the national psyche, a passionate, chaotic blend of individual brilliance, improvisation, and emotional intensity. Diego Maradona's dribbling against England in the 1986 World Cup is often described as a perfect representation of Argentine artistry.[4] His ability to weave through the English defense with fluidity and elegance was a moment that transcended sport, akin to a dancer performing an impromptu piece on stage. The Argentine game is heralded as an art form. It prioritizes flair, creativity, and dramatic moments, as exemplified by Maradona's "Hand of God" goal or his solo run against England. These moments of raw artistry, where the boundaries of strategy blur into emotional marvel, reflect the paidia aspect of football: moments of unstructured brilliance that defy the constraints of the formal game.

During Barcelona's 2015 Champions League match against Bayern Munich, Lionel Messi's dribble past Jerome Boateng, followed by a delicate chip over Manuel Neuer, became a testament to his genius and his ability to create moments of pure art in the middle of intense competition. This moment, touching the sublime, perfectly encapsulates the type of individual brilliance Argentina nurtures—an expression of raw, unbridled creativity in a game often dictated by structure and organization.

By contrast, the Dutch approach, particularly during the "Total Football" era in the 1970s, leans more toward a design philosophy. Spearheaded by Johan Cruyff and Rinus Michels, Total Football is a system of positional fluidity, tactical innovation, and team coordination.[5] Total Football is like the paintings of Piet Mondrian, whose abstract compositions focus on harmony and balance rather than spontaneous, emotional expression. It is a vision of football where every player is involved in both offensive and defensive responsibilities, where the system itself is as important as the individual within it. In a match against Brazil during the 1974 World Cup, Johan Cruyff orchestrated a play known as the "Cruyff Turn". The move, executed within the framework of the team's fluid movement, emphasized not only technical brilliance but also the precision and balance inherent to the Dutch design. The Dutch game is less about the individual's moment of spontaneous smartness and more about the harmony of a designed, collective structure, what we might consider football as a form of ludus. While Total Football is celebrated for its creativity and innovation, it does so within the framework of tactical discipline, making it a game that values design as much as expression.

GLOBAL AND LOCAL

Football's globalization began with colonial and industrial forces, as the game spread worldwide through British imperial expansion and industrialization.[6] However, its spread was never a one-way transmission of a static model. Instead, football was adapted and reinterpreted according to each country's cultural and social conditions. This adaptation process was especially visible in South America, where football's introduction by British expatriates and elites quickly became a working-class passion, reshaped by local values, as seen in Brazil's rise of the "samba football" style. In Italy, defensive tactics like *catenaccio* mirrored the country's sociopolitical landscape, emphasizing pragmatism and strategic control.

Football is a game of exploring and exploiting space, a dynamic, real-time negotiation of presence, pressure, and potential. Every match is a cartography of movement, a lived and constantly shifting map where players navigate and redraw lines of control. It is colonization not in the historical sense of imperial conquest, but a moment-to-moment spatial strategy in which territory is claimed, lost, and reclaimed within the strict but fluid architecture of the pitch and the rules that govern it. The field is both grid and battlefield, where the dominator and victim are not fixed roles but oscillating positions vulnerable to instant reversal. A momentary lapse in structure, awareness, or an exceptional display of skill can invert the balance of power and redraw the contours of dominance.

This strategic grammar of space, the reading, sensing, and manipulating of it, is not universal. It has evolved differently across cultures, terrains, and sociohistorical contexts. Football is not merely played in different countries; it is interpreted differently, inscribed with the physical, social, and material conditions of its environment. The possibility space of football is shaped as much by local circumstance and training culture as by global rule sets.

The origins of the English game are deeply tied to a particular geography and institutional setting: the muddy meadows, grassy commons, and makeshift pitches on the outskirts of boarding schools, village greens, and civic yards. These relatively open spaces encouraged a style of play focused on long balls, territorial gain, and quick physical transitions up and down the flanks. Here, football became a game of conquering space, covering ground, launching attacks down the wings, and physically imposing oneself on an opponent. It is a form of linear spatial colonization, where the path to dominance is a matter of acceleration and reach—get it forward, move fast, take ground.

By contrast, the Dutch game was forged in a denser, more spatially constrained environment. Urbanization, scarcity of large open playing fields, and a different relationship to space necessitated a different reading of the game. Here, football developed more like a dance of compression and expansion, where close quarters and constant pressure demanded technical precision, positional awareness, and a collective sense of movement. Space wasn't something to conquer in long strides; it was something to negotiate, pass by pass, with the opponent often just a few feet away. If the English style evokes colonial expansion, the Dutch style is urban warfare; an art of survival in tight spaces, of coordinated, systemic responses to limited room for maneuver.

These different spatial grammars reflect more than tactical preference. They embody distinct definitions of the game, a set of differing ontologies of football. They tell us how players are trained to perceive space, how they are habituated to move within it, and what kinds of intelligence are valued: brute physicality or fluid positionality; individuality or collectivity; straight lines or triangulated webs.

Brazilian football is defined by its artistry, flair, and emphasis on individual expression.[7] Brazilian players, from Pelé to Ronaldo to Vinicius Junior, have embodied a style of play that prioritizes ingenuity, improvisation, and skill. "Samba football"—or *ginga* as they call it—is characterized by fluid ball control, dazzling dribbles, and a relaxed, free-flowing approach to the game. The focus is less on rigid tactical discipline and more on allowing players to express themselves on the field, creating magical moments that captivate both players and spectators alike. This approach is deeply rooted in Brazil's cultural fabric, where football has been synonymous with national pride and identity. Brazilian football is shaped by its history of poverty, where the streets and beaches served as training grounds for future stars. The emphasis on improvisation reflects a broader cultural value placed on personal flair, rhythm, and artistic expression. When a Brazilian player pulls off a bicycle kick or a samba-style dribble, they are not only showcasing their technical skill but also enacting a form of national cultural pride.

The Germans have historically emphasized discipline, tactical organization, and collective play. The German approach to football is built on the philosophy of *Mannschaft* (teamwork) and is often exemplified by a focus on efficiency and tactical structure. The German national team's approach is methodical, emphasizing defensive solidity and well-coordinated team movements, which reflect the broader cultural values of order and collective effort. The influence of German football can be traced back to the postwar period, where the sport mirrored the country's economic and social rebuilding, *die Wirtschaftswunder*, the miracle of business. German football's success in tournaments is often attributed to its disciplined approach, with each player understanding their role within a system designed to maximize team effectiveness. Unlike Brazil, where individual flair is celebrated, Germany's football style places a premium on coordinated movement, strategic positioning, and the ability to execute plans with near mechanical precision.

As the birthplace of modern football, England's approach, as already mentioned, is deeply rooted in tradition and a balance between physicality and skill. English football is known for its fast-paced nature, focus on direct play, and an emphasis on physical strength and endurance. The Premier League showcases a more traditional style of play with an emphasis on athleticism, high pressing, and set-piece mastery. However, over time, there has been a growing emphasis on tactical flexibility, influenced by continental European styles. English football has had an ambivalent relationship with continental tactical innovations, often preferring a more direct and confrontational approach. In recent decades, the Premier League has seen the infusion of international styles, incorporating elements of possession-based football alongside its traditionally more rugged approach. This ongoing evolution reflects the country's complex relationship with its footballing heritage and the globalizing forces that shape the modern game.

Italian football has long been associated with *catenaccio*, a highly defensive tactical system that emphasizes tight organization, counterattacking, and a robust defense-first philosophy. The cultural value of *catenaccio* reflects Italy's sociopolitical landscape, where pragmatism and control often take precedence over flamboyance. Catholicism, one could say, plays a role here: players, like congregants, cheat a little bit, cunningly and clever, and get absolution. The Italian national team has been known for its ability to adapt to various styles, but its heart lies in a tactical approach where the primary goal is to neutralize the opposition's strengths and wait for the opportunity to strike on the counter. This defensive emphasis mirrors the Italian ethos of balance and resilience, where defense is seen as an art form. *Catenaccio* was most famously employed by Inter Milan under Helenio Herrera in the 1960s, and it has continued to influence Italian football at both the club and national levels. While the game in Italy has evolved over time to include more offensive tactics, the core of Italian football remains grounded in defensive mastery and tactical discipline.

Spain's football style is often associated with tiqui-taca, a system of short passing, intricate ball movement, and a focus on maintaining possession. This approach is rooted in the Spanish emphasis on technical skill, particularly through players like Xavi Hernández, Andrés Iniesta, and Sergio Busquets, who embody a system that values precision and collective harmony. The success of the Spanish national team, particularly during their golden era from 2008 to 2012, exemplified the effectiveness of tiqui-taca, where sustained possession allowed Spain to wear down opponents and control the tempo of the game. Spanish football's technical emphasis is rooted in its historical and cultural context. The La Masia academy at FC Barcelona has been instrumental in developing a style that prioritizes technique over physicality, teaching players to see the field as a space for controlled artistry. The approach is highly systematized and reflects Spain's value of artistic expression through a shared team dynamic.

Football is often framed by cultural clichés, so the above simplistic narratives do not always reflect the reality of how the game has evolved or how teams have approached tactical innovation. For example, Brazil is frequently depicted as the epitome of samba football, celebrated for its improvisational style. This image completely overlooks Brazil's historical tactical sophistication. As early as the 1958 World Cup in Sweden, Brazil adopted the 4-2-4 formation, a highly organized system that balanced attacking flair with defensive structure. Brazil's use of zonal marking and tactical discipline in defense, often seen as antithetical to the notion of free play, further demonstrates that Brazilian football has been shaped by individual creativity and strategic thinking. This blend of technical artistry and tactical awareness is a defining feature of Brazil's footballing legacy.

Similarly, the stereotype of Norway's "boring" football under Eigil "Drillo" Olsen has been widely circulated. Drillo coached Norway from 1990 to 1998. The team's long-ball style, criticized for lacking flair, was viewed as a retreat into defensive pragmatism. However, this characterization fails to acknowledge the tactical genius of Olsen's 4-5-1 system, which, while seemingly conservative, became highly influential in European football. The defensive solidity and disciplined structure of Drillo's approach were not only effective but also widely adopted by other teams, most notably by José Mourinho's Chelsea side in the early 2000s which deployed a 4-1-4-1 formation with Claude Makélélé as controlling midfielder. Far from being boring, the Norwegian strategy was a precursor to modern tactical formations that emphasize control and counterattacking, reflecting a broader trend in the evolution of football tactics.

THE POSSIBILITY SPACE

Formations—like Italian Carlo Ancelotti's "christmas tree", 4-3-2-1, which he used in AC Milan around 2007, or Drillo's much-maligned 4-5-1—are only surface numerals for the same deeper game. They script initial positions and roles, but what coaches and players actually manage is a shifting field of affordances created by the Laws of the Game, the ball, and 22 moving bodies. In Oslo or Naples, Buenos Aires or Birmingham, the local dialects differ—pressing heights, rest-defense shapes, trigger cues—but they all draw from (and rejoice in) the same underlying possibility space. While numbers name a pre-kickoff arrangement, possibility space names what those numbers can become: pressure lines that tilt, passing lanes that open and shut, cover shadows that morph into traps, and decoys that turn into third-man runs. Read this way, "systems" are not templates to be copied but lenses to perceive and manipulate options. The point is not which formation you choose, but how you continuously convert positions into options as the game updates from moment to moment.

"Possibility space" in a mathematical or geometric context refers to the set of all possible outcomes or configurations of a given system, defined by the parameters that describe the system's state. In this book we use possibility space to mean the realm of actions the laws of football make available at any instant, and the ways players and coaches continually explore that realm. It's geometric (a 105 × 68 meter grid), kinetic (movements, accelerations, flight paths), and temporal (beats, delays, disguises). Positions are only the surface. What matters is how positions become options. A marking angle turns into a press, and a touch buys just enough time for depth to appear.

Because the game updates every fraction of a second, each decision pushes the match into a new "state", opening some corridors while closing others. Possibility space is therefore not an abstract infinity but a lived calculus. Affordances emerge, vanish, and reappear as the rules, the ball, and 22 bodies interact. Two quick snapshots show how this works.

Consider Liverpool–Barcelona at Anfield in 2019, the men's game. At 3-0 on the night and 3-3 on aggregate, Trent Alexander-Arnold notices a defensive lapse at a corner: Barcelona are organizing for a routine delivery; Divock Origi has slipped into a pocket near the penalty spot. The laws are simple—the ball must be stationary in the quadrant; the taker may restart when ready—but within that tight frame the tempo is negotiable. Alexander-Arnold feints to walk away, then whips the corner early. One micro-decision flips the state of the match: inattentive zonal markers become statues; an unmarked finisher becomes inevitable. The possibility space didn't expand. It tilted because time was used as a tactical dimension.

Now shift to the women's game: England–Germany, Euro 2022 final at Wembley. Keira Walsh receives the ball under light pressure in the center circle and, with a quick glance, threads a diagonal through-ball between center-backs for Ella Toone's curving run. Offside law draws a bright line; Toone rides it, adjusting her movement so the pass meets her onside, then lifts a first-time chip over the keeper. Here, the constraint (offside) doesn't suppress invention; it shapes it. The run's angle, the pass's power, the finish's finesse, these are three precise choices, one open corridor. England didn't invent a new move; they navigated the existing map perfectly. The lesson is the same. Possibility space is the meeting point of rules and imagination, of ludus and paidea. Recalling Caillois' concepts, what we have here is agon, the competitive battle between "fences", as Huizinga would say. Alea is also reflected: near post, far post, hitting the crossbar, the ball goes in, or it deflects and jumps wide. And since the possibility space is a lawful construction that invites cunning (think of the Italians), mimicry is involved. On top of that, it can make the players as well as you, the observer, dizzy (*ilinx*). As managers try to narrow it into repeatable patterns, players keep finding seams that patterns can't quite close. That is why football remains inexhaustible; not because anything can happen, but because, within strict limits, the game continually discovers new ways for the right thing to happen.

The concept of possibility space is so central to our understanding of football that we have an entire chapter dedicated to it (Chapter 4). We have just introduced it here as a way of situating the tension between ludus and paideia and how that can reflect the global and the local in football. But we haven't exhausted what this concept can do for understanding football, and we will return to it in depth later in the book.

EINSTEIN ON THE PITCH

"You have to learn the rules of the game. And then you have to play better than anyone else", Albert Einstein once said. Rules establish the structure within the game—a clear system that players must follow. However, the structure isn't a fixed set of limitations, nor is it reversible like in standard physics. Instead, it forms a dynamic environment that enables endless creative variation. The potential space, therefore, is an emergent property of the game. It cannot be fully predicted or controlled, but emerges from the interactions between players, the field, the ball, and the rules. Players explore this space through decisions like when to pass, where to position themselves, or how to approach the opposition. Each choice guides the game in a new direction, creating new states that didn't exist before. What makes this even more fascinating is the nonlinear nature of the potential space. Unlike a game with fixed steps or outcomes, football allows for an almost infinite range of results from any given moment. When a player passes the ball, the choice of recipient, the timing of the pass, and the defending reactions generate a nearly limitless array of possible outcomes. In a video game, such scenarios might be limited by preset decision trees or algorithms, but in football, human intuition, skill, and improvisation continuously generate a series of evolving options.

The tactical assessments that define the game's trajectory—such as choosing when to apply pressure or retreat—create branching pathways within the possibility space. The decisions made by individual players at any given moment reverberate through the entire system, often with cascading effects that can shift the momentum of the game or completely alter its outcome. The most intriguing aspect of this is that the game's outcome is not predetermined; the possibility space is not only a theoretical space but a tangible one, shaped by each action. No two games are alike, as each encounter uniquely manifests the interplay between structure and spontaneity.

NARROWNESS

Before we close this chapter, let's talk about *narrowness*. Football is a tactical game that seeks to "narrow" the possibility space, meaning the range of possible actions or outcomes, into a manageable set of probabilities. The hope is that this will lead to the most effective way to win. Teams and players use various tactical systems, formations, and strategies to limit opponents' options while maximizing their own. The goal is to reduce the game's uncertainty, structuring it so that decisions can be made with the highest likelihood of success. In this sense, the game transforms the open-ended possibilities of play into a probability space, where the most likely paths to victory are calculated through strategy, positioning, and decision-making.

Josep "Pep" Guardiola, manager of Manchester City, believes in a style of football where players are free to roam the spaces between the zones. He calls it "positional play".[8] The pitch is split into zones, with each player assigned a zone. Each movement triggers a chain reaction, setting off the movement of a teammate to confuse the opposition. Players are programmed to manipulate the right spaces and apply pressure in certain areas. In short, they need to be flexible. This is exactly what narrowing is about: it enables teams to control the flow of the match and increase their chances of securing a win. Narrowness is the tactical capacity to transform the open-ended expanse of possibilities into a linear trajectory that hopefully leads to victory. Except, of course, when it doesn't.

At its core, football is a dynamic field where players push against the boundaries set by the rules to create infinite tactical variations, artistic expressions, and emotional moments. Globalization has ensured that universal rules like the offside law govern football's fundamental framework—1925 is a landmark—and team structure remains constant. At the same time, however, as we saw earlier, the possibility space of football is constantly transformed by different countries' cultural, social, and historical contexts. From Brazil's ginga, where flair and improvisation dominate, to Germany's *Gegenpress* and Italy's defensive mastery—and to Denmark, where long-serving coach Morten Olsen popularized the idiosyncratic coinage "automatisms" to describe what he thought football was about—each nation brings its own tenet to the game, deducing the global rules through a local lens.

All these national styles and ways of being passionate about the game leave their mark on fandom, both light and dark. "Football is popular because stupidity is popular", the Argentinian writer Jorge Luis Borges said.[9] He even scheduled one of his lectures so that it would intentionally conflict with Argentina's first game of the 1978 World Cup. Fans interpret the possibility space in different ways, and their engagement with the game—whether through the passionate chants and songs that echo through English stadiums, the dramatic pyrotechnics in Italy and South America, or the more subdued appreciation in other parts of Europe—adds an additional layer of dynamism to the sport. This is not simply a spectator sport; it is a cultural phenomenon. It's a deadly serious culture; yet, it's also funny when looked at from the outside, as the late Umberto Eco did in *How to Travel with a Salmon and Other Essays*, from 1994: "I don't like the football fan, because he has a strange defect: he cannot understand why you are not a fan yourself, and he insists on talking to you as if you were". Eco comes across a taxi driver convinced that every other human being is also a fan. How can it be that creatures are "so adamantine in their conviction that all humans are the same" and "ready to bash in the head of the fan who comes from the neighboring province", Eco asks. This version of "ecumenical chauvinism", in Eco's words, contributes to the game's living, breathing atmosphere. In different corners of the world, the interpretation of a match varies drastically from the exhilaration of a goal scored in Brazil's Maracanã, with samba beats and fireworks filling the air, to the calculated celebration of a well-executed counterattack in Bayern München's Allianz Arena.

But the football landscape is changing, and as we continue to advance into the digital age, the introduction of artificial intelligence (AI) and automation into the game is set to drastically alter the nature of football, its practice, and its fandom. AI and automation are already beginning to shape the game through advanced analytics, tactical simulations, and performance optimization. Coaches and teams increasingly use AI-driven data to refine player performance, scout new talent, and predict match outcomes, creating a more scientific approach to the game. From video assistant referees (VAR) that assist in decision-making to AI algorithms that help with tactical planning and injury prevention, technology is infiltrating football at all levels. And so, we will ask in the remainder of this book, framed by game studies and biased through the lens of Eco's ecumenical taxi driver: will football become a more mechanized and predictable sport, with AI algorithms shaping every pass, every movement, and every decision? Or will it retain its fundamental unpredictability, with players and teams from all around the world continuing to push against the constraints of technology to create moments of pure human brilliance?

NOTES

1 Roger Caillois: *Man, Play and Games.* University of Illinois Press, 1961 [1958].
2 Recall the word "protagonist" means in Greek the first fighter to appear on stage.
3 IFAB: *Laws of the Game.* Zürich: International Football Association Board, updated annually. For a history of the offside law: Mike Collett: *The Complete Record of the FA Cup.* SportsBooks, 2003.
4 Jonathan Wilson: *Angels with Dirty Faces: How Argentinian Soccer Defined a Nation and Changed the Game Forever.* Orion, 2016.
5 Jonathan Wilson: *Inverting the Pyramid: The History of Football Tactics.* Orion, 2008. See especially the chapters on Michels and Cruyff.
6 David Goldblatt: *The Ball Is Round: A Global History of Football.* Penguin, 2007.
7 Paulo Fontes and Bernardo Buarque de Hollanda (Eds.): *The Country of Football: Politics, Popular Culture, and the Beautiful Game in Brazil.* University Press of Florida, 2014.
8 Martí Perarnau: *Pep Confidential: The Inside Story of Pep Guardiola's First Season at Bayern Munich.* Arena Sport, 2014.
9 Jorge Luis Borges: "El fútbol a sol y sombra." In *Obras completas.* Emecé, 1989. For fandom and culture: Richard Giulianotti: *Football: A Sociology of the Global Game.* Polity, 1999.

CHAPTER 2

The Beautiful Rule

When the legendary Manchester United manager Sir Alex Ferguson faced A.C. Milan in the 1990s, he was always aware of the perils of encountering the Italian striker Filippo "Pippo" Inzaghi. Not because he was fast, or particularly strong, or a technical genius. Inzaghi was a master of being almost, but not quite, offside. His most remarkable talent was timing at the edge of the game. In a classic goal against Bayern München in October 2002,[1] Inzaghi cleverly held his position offside before swiftly sprinting behind the defensive line to score. This goal, like many others from Inzaghi's career, highlights the thrilling nature of the offside rule—the most captivating rule in the beautiful game.

What makes football "the beautiful game"? Regular answers will probably praise athletic effort, movement of bodies, and the unique skills that defy the impossibility of getting a ball to do what we want it to do with our feet. All of these points are valid, and attempting to answer that silly question only serves to reduce football to the vocabulary of aesthetics. Nonetheless, it is an interesting question. In this chapter, we will take a different route. As game scholars, we often focus on what defines *a game*. One of the defining characteristics of games is that they are rule-based activities. Therefore, the

DOI: 10.1201/9781003636762-3

questions here will be simple: what makes a rule beautiful, and are games with beautiful rules themselves beautiful?

This chapter examines the concept of game beauty, using football as a case study. The game studies ideas we are introducing come from a close reading of game philosopher Thi Nguyen's argument that games are the art form of agency.[2] Nguyen argues that game rules are form of transmitting agencies, ways of acting in the world. Games are not the only modes of transmitting forms of agency; however, games are the aesthetic form of creating and transmitting forms of agency through rules. Our approach consists of a two-step process. First, we will explain Nguyen's argument about beauty and games. Then we will apply that argument to game rules. By the end of the chapter, we will have illustrated how the rules of a game can be beautiful and why the offside rule is the most beautiful rule of them all.

ART, GAMES, RULES

One of the classic questions in the field of game studies is whether games are art. We believe that every reader may have an answer to that particular question, but we think it's essential to use football as a means to understand whether games are part of the arts. But that's a misleading question. We should not ask whether games are art, but rather how games create aesthetic experiences. A good starting point, outside game studies, will be the philosophy of sports. Author David Best[3] argued that some sports are similar to the arts "(…) in that their purpose cannot be considered apart from the manner of achieving it" (p. 480). What does this mean? Essentially, we should consider whether playing a game is also aesthetically pleasing. It does not matter if we socially consider the game to be art or not. Art is a social construction, an agreement within cultures about what phenomena we consider aesthetically worthy. What matters is whether playing a game is an activity of aesthetic value. That's what we are discussing here: is football a game in which the way of playing is as important as achieving the goals of the game, and therefore, it is an aesthetically relevant game? We think that football is such a game, and that's what we are going to be explaining in the following pages. Intuitively, anybody who has watched Messi's free kicks or Hope Solo's impossible saves, or who has scored a top corner goal in a Sunday league match, knows of the beauty of the game. But where does that aesthetic pleasure come from?

That question has occupied game studies almost since the inception of academic game studies.[4] Most aesthetic theories of games should be understood as aesthetic theories of *gameplay*, that is, studies of how playing (or watching) a game can lead to an aesthetic experience. In the game studies tradition, the beauty of games is often associated with the performance of players during gameplay. See for example this quote by sports philosopher Elcombe:[5]

> *We create, return to, adjust, watch, discuss, mythologize physical games because they appeal to us in a significant, embodied sense; because a game that revolves around putting a leather ball into a metal hoop ten feet off the ground is, when considered on aesthetic rather than mechanical or coldly informational grounds, potentially a deeply meaningful practice created by humans for humans.*

In *What We Think About When We Think About Football*,[6] Simon Critchley made a compelling argument about the importance of the experience of football as a source of aesthetic experiences: "The phenomenological approach will lead us into a poetics of time, space, drama and all the elements of what William James calls 'this mysterious sensorial life' that make up the varieties of football experience".

Most analyses of the aesthetics of games, then, have focused on the games being played, on the beauty of action for players and spectators, and on the movement and patterns of action.[7] This is the dominant way of thinking about the aesthetics of games, but it does leave out a fundamental question: what characteristics does a game have, as an object, to create that particular beauty? Since all games have rules, it would be interesting to consider the role of rules in creating the aesthetic experiences of play.

That's why, in this chapter, we adapt Nguyen's theory of games and art. Nguyen understands that games are "a method for inscribing forms of agency into artifactual vessels [...] games [...] communicate forms of agency" (p. 1). We need to examine *how* games inscribe agency to understand their aesthetic value. Since games utilize rules to modify agency, we can consider rules as having aesthetic value. And therefore, we can consider regulations to have a form of beauty in themselves.

Without spoiling the rest of the chapter, let us give an example, starting with the relation between agency and rules. In football, there is a rule that states only the goalkeeper can use their hands to touch the ball during play

(Law 12). This rule defines the agency of players in football. It also helps us explain the magnetic beauty of seeing Zidane, Ronaldinho, or Marta *follow that rule*. What extraordinary players can do with their feet, some of us can only dream of doing with our hands. It's as if those players appropriated that rule to demonstrate that playing football can be like dancing.

Let us give another example. The laws of the game stipulate that the goalkeeper is the only player allowed to pick up the ball with their hands. Until 1992, that rule also included back passes. That is, a defender could pass back to their goalkeeper, who would then pick up the ball with their hands. This is a flawed rule, and if you don't believe us, try watching any match from the 1990 World Cup. Or, we're sorry to say, much of the second half of the 1992 EuroCup final that Denmark won—their team was constantly passing legendary goalkeeper Peter Schmeichel the ball, so he could pick it up with his hands, wait a little bit, and make a long pass. The title of European Champion for Denmark was also a somewhat unintended outcome of that rule.

Alarmed by the lack of beauty of those early 1990s games, FIFA decided to modify the goalkeeper rule just slightly: now, goalkeepers could not pick up the ball if the pass came from their own team. Suddenly, goalkeepers needed to play like field players! Something that, in fairness, the Dutch school of Rinus Michels and Johan Cruyff had already advocated for. That subtle rule change modified the agency of goalkeepers. It gave us a phenomenal new understanding of what being a goalkeeper entails, illustrated by the likes of Bayern München's Manuel Neuer or Spain's Cata Coll, whose calm passing in the 2023 Women's World Cup Final helped overcome the relentless English pressing game.

What we are arguing is simple: we can talk about the aesthetic value of rules if we connect them to how they shape agency during gameplay. How rules shape agency, creating behaviors while also remaining open to creative interpretation and appropriation, are elements that qualify the aesthetic value of a rule. Rules enable the beauty of the game as played. Let's apply this argument to the offside rule in football.

THINKING ABOUT THE BEAUTY OF THE OFFSIDE RULE

Football at its highest level can occasionally look like a choreographed contest. High-pressing teams, such as Klopp's Liverpool or the English Women's National Team, move their midfield and defensive lines together, choking the opposition and forcing them to make mistakes that lead to quick passes and shots on goal. Occasionally, this high pressure leads to a striker breaking the defensive line and running alone toward the goal, having found a space that did not exist there before, racing to score a one-on-one duel with the goalkeeper. Football is a game of collective action and individual brilliance. The offside rule is beautiful because it ties individual prowess to collective effort, while also affecting the space in which the game is played and the role of referees. It is a simple rule that meaningfully affects all levels of the game, and that's why it is beautiful. Let's look at these effects in more detail.

Individual Level

A reasonable rule constraints what we can do when playing a game, while creating meaningful action to reach a particular goal. As we mentioned earlier, the central rule of football, which only allows the foot to be used to move the ball on the pitch, is what makes playing the game both fun and challenging. Good rules encourage play by developing skills and overcoming challenges. Rules should then be evaluated following two parameters: for the individual player, how does a rule constrain agency in a meaningful way, and how does the rule allow for pleasurable forms of play within its bounds? The offside rule presents a clear challenge that players can overcome by developing a particular skill set: a player must be able to read the opponent's defensive line and time their runs so they don't incur an offside foul.

We opened this chapter by invoking the figure of the Italian forward Filippo Inzaghi, one of the best examples of how the offside rule can create beauty in football. Inzaghi was not the most technically gifted of strikers, nor the fastest. Inzaghi excelled at being always barely onside, reading the timing of the defense and of the passes to make perfect attacking runs. Inzaghi has an excellent track record: the seventh-highest scorer in Italy, a two-time Champions League winner, and a three-time Italian Champion. All of that built on the unique talent of being on-time, onside, and attacking the ball with the right timing. Inzaghi understood football as a game of time and space, always on the limit.

But the offside rule is not just crucial for attacking players. It is fair to say that no player can become a professional if they don't have the timing skills to *play* the offside rule. A defender needs to be able to tackle opponents, as well as help draw a defensive line that can trap attackers offside. Another Italian legend, Franco Baresi, could arguably be the defensive equivalent of

Inzaghi: Baresi's most remarkable talent was his reading of time and space to perform offside traps in the risky defensive systems of coach Arrigo Sacchi. Sacchi liked to play with a high defensive line, pushing the opposing team far away from their goal as an extra layer of defense. To achieve this, Sacchi trusted Baresi's leadership and timing. These skills enabled him to quickly identify an opponent who could be offside and move to draw the line, thereby placing the player offside and voiding the threat.

Inzhagui and Baresi, the striker and the defender, their careers are a testament to how the offside rule shapes the skills and actions of football players, demonstrating how reading space, time, and collective movements can make a difference in the game of margins that is football played at its highest level.

Collective Level

Football is a team sport. Any argument about the beauty of the rule needs to take into consideration not only how it encourages and develops specific player skills, but also how it has an effect in the way teams play. As mentioned, one of Baresi's most extraordinary talents was his capacity to lead a defense line that would regularly catch opponents in an offside trap. The rule creates a form of collective agency, providing the framing, purpose, and structure for the development of strategies that require the coordination of players so that they behave as one, throwing the defensive line up the pitch simultaneously to catch opposing players in an offside position.

Part of the aesthetic value of team sports resides in these moments of collective agency that go beyond the individual skills of a player. A game facilitates instances of coordination between players that together form a distinct, distributed, and multiple-agent system: a team.

The offside rule then facilitates collective action. But it also creates a mesmerizing spectacle, that of the player against a team. If the player is like Inzaghi, they will identify a weak link in the defense line's setup and exploit it. If the team has the coordination of Sacchi's mythical Milan, the attacker will never stand a chance. A lone striker, perched at the edge of the offside line, waiting for the right time, while the opposing team is moving as a block, moving the attacker back and forth as a piece of wood in the waves. It's a physical as well as a mental challenge, a game of patience, of one against many that act as one.

Material Level

Football is a game played by too few players on a too large pitch. The offside rule allows for the actual space where the game is played to be of variable size, dynamically changing the material conditions of the game. The variable size of the play area depends on the movements of teams and individuals. In other words, the defensive and offensive lines determine the actual size of the pitch on which the game is played. While the pitch may be officially 100 meters or more, the actual game is played only within the 30–60 meters between the defensive lines. That space shifts as teams move, effectively altering the size of the pitch as the game progresses.

While playing the offside trap can be an effective way to compress the playing field and allow for more efficient pressing, it is also vulnerable to speedy attackers who thrive on timed runs. The offside rule adds another layer of aesthetic value to the game of football, connecting the individual and the collective to the material conditions of play. The offside rule encourages players to play with the pitch itself, adding dynamism to the concept of football as a game of space and time.

Rule Management Level

What is a rule suitable for if it is not enforced? Enforcing Law 11 depends explicitly on referee judgment. If we are to be very technical about things, the offside rule defines a state that can lead to an offense only when a player is behind the second-to-last defender at the moment a pass *intended* to reach them is made. Then, and only then, there is an offside offense. The offense is then called by a human referee, who evaluates whether the player was offside at the moment the pass was sent and whether the player showed interest in continuing the play. A player can be offside, but there is no offense if they do not want to follow the play. A player can be offside, but if their position does not interfere with the goalkeeper's line of sight, there is no offense. A player could have an arm in a slightly advanced position and not trigger an offside offense.

The offside rule was designed to depend on referees' interpretations of a player's position and intention during play. The rule is relatively straightforward regarding when a player is offside, but it leaves some wiggle room for interpretation. Unlike the rule that defines what a goal is (the ball crossing the entire goal line completely), the offside rule requires interpretation.

Referees need to read the play as it happens, and in doing so, the rule adds another layer of agency-driven aesthetic value. The referee must exercise judgment to apply the rule.

The role of interpreting and enforcing rules adds a layer of agency to the game that is not present in many of the other laws of football. Law 11 has an impact on how the referee interprets the rules, the flow of play, and the specific timing of situations. At the same time, it affects how players can act and behave toward the run of play, for example, by actively showing that they are not part of the game, so that the referee cannot interpret them as actively participating in the sequence of play. The importance of interpretation, as stated in Law 11, gives referees and players an additional domain where they have agency, specifically related to understanding the rules as the game is played.

We call football "the beautiful game", but that's a hard sell for those who only see a slow game with almost no points scored, played on a fairly large pitch in which teams spread out so much that it's not possible to fit all of them in a panoramic camera shot.[8] Even for casual players, football can be challenging, as you seldom get relevant time on the ball and quite often have to take a sprint that leads nowhere. And yet, football is the world's sport, a spectacle that for billions is mesmerizing to watch.

MATTERS OF BEAUTY

It's time to take a step back from football and think from the perspective of game studies. What we've done in this chapter is argue that the beauty of a game is a consequence not only of how the game is played, but also of the rules of that game. We have also argued that some rules can be described as genuinely beautiful due to the ways they impact individual and collective agency, and how they also allow for interpretation and subtlety in their implementation. Nguyen argues that games are the art form of agency because they contain forms of agency that we can inhabit. Those forms of agency have a series of starting points: the presence of players, the location for the play experience, the social context and relations between players, and the rules of the game.

Football is beautiful in motion, when played, in its social, embodied, and cultural dynamism. That motion originates from voluntary adherence to its rules, whether the official rules emanating from FIFA or the regulations determined by the collective decision of players in a park on any given sunny Sunday. We should understand the aesthetic beauty of a rule when we consider how it creates or limits agency, how it enables players to act in particular ways, or how it prevents specific forms of action.

Game studies would argue that the offside rule is beautiful because of the ways it generates individual, collective, material, and interpretative modes of agency that define the aesthetic qualities of the sport as it is played, as we just saw. If games are the art form of agency, rules can be considered as artistic expressions when they provide multiple forms of agency that are put in practice in the act of playing a game. This is the key contribution to the field of game studies: for a rule to be considered aesthetically relevant, it should *minimally* affect the individual agency of a player as experienced in the context of gameplay. At the same time, it should have a maximum effect on both the material and interpretive layers of the game.

Because we are doing game studies research, we should argue how these ideas can be extended beyond the offside rule. For example, the basketball rule that prevents attacking players to pass the ball back to their side of the court has similar effects than the offside rule: it encourages dynamism in individual agency as well as in collective agency, and it has an impact in the material practice of the game; plus, it is up to the referees to determine the intention of a defensive player when the ball crosses the half-court line. A good exercise in understanding the aesthetic beauty of games is to translate the template we have used here to examine rules, asking ourselves: how does this rule affect individual agency? How does it affect collective agency? How does it affect the material conditions of the game, such as the pitch or the objects we use to play, from sticks to balls? And, finally, is the rule open for interpretation while the game is being played?

There's one last thing we want to discuss here. We have intentionally omitted the fact that at the highest levels of the game, the referee is now assisted by a video review system that can help draw the offside lines and determine whether a player was offside when receiving the ball. The application of video assisted refereeing (VAR) to help referees make decisions in top-flight football has been a contentious issue since the very start.[9] While the idea of referees being assisted by other referees armed with monitors, video, and artificial intelligence was sold as a triumph of fairness,[10] the outcomes have been extremely controversial. Few football fans seem to think that VAR has been an unequivocally good addition to the beautiful game.

The VAR application has had an impact on the handball rule, the duration of matches, and the collective joy of celebrating a goal. Attending a game at a stadium now is a strange affair: your team scores, you cheer, and then wait to make sure that cheering was the correct response. Sometimes, you get to cheer twice. Sometimes, VAR shows that what we all understood to be a goal, from the stands to the sidelines, was offside. It's a weird, odd, diffuse form of cheering. For many football fans, there is an ineffable *something* that is wrong with VAR, something that shows a clash between the theoretical benefits of applying technology (fairness) and the actual practical effects of its application.[11]

Let us propose an argument to explain this failure of technology. VAR promises fairness through the objective application of the rules. Objectivity is "guaranteed" by the combination of the truth mode of video and artificial intelligence with the time given to referees to observe, in high definition detail and with pause, the events in the game.[12] However, VAR is being applied to a rule designed to be open for interpretation. Is the player offside when the pass is sent? Which part of the player? Are they gaining an advantage? Are they blocking the view of the goalkeeper? Those are questions the referee needs to answer and make a decision during the run of the game. An arm, a hand, or even a foot can be offside, but it does not necessarily give an attacker an unfair advantage. The lines drawn by computer-aided software indicate positions. Still, ultimately, the referee should decide whether an arm, elbow, or head gives a player an unfair advantage.

In late 2025, the IFAB discussed a change to the offside rule proposed by legendary coach Arsene Wenger. To make the rule clearer, less prone to mistakes, and to increase scoring in matches, Wenger suggested that a player is only offside if all of their body parts overlap with a defender. No more calls based on an arm or toe being offside. When writing this, the rule change has not yet been adopted. However, Wenger's idea highlights the challenges of applying technology to a rule meant to be vague and based on human judgment, not computer analysis.

With VAR, the interpretive aesthetic quality of the rule is slowly substituted by a technical solution that implements logics of computational evaluation through technology.[13] Football has evolved to be an unfair game, a game with fallibility at heart, due to the importance of interpretation.[14] The commercial interests surrounding the top-flight game are in contradiction with that fallibility, requiring a technology of capital to ensure that potential human error does not harm the "objective" results.

Yet the aesthetic pleasure of the game derives partially from the fact that some decisions about the run of the game, the shape and size of the pitch, and the intentions of others are up for human interpretation. The aesthetics of football are not limited to the moments of athletic prowess; the game is beautiful when Maradona scores a clearly illegal goal that the referee does not see, or when Filippo Inzaghi is so close to being offside that it is impossible to decide whether he is on or offside. Football is aesthetically valuable when it is a flowing clash of individual and collective action in a variably sized play space within a larger pitch, all regulated by a fallible human interpreting and applying the law.

The beauty of football lies in its proximity to ritual and law: it depends on a person's deliberation, on direct engagement with an authority that can be wrong. This is not an unfair game, but it is profoundly human. VAR brings inhuman power to the game, a logic of fairness rooted in economic interests. VAR introduces a logic of computation into the gaming experience. Because of the interpretive space created by the offside rule, football fully explores the limits of human agency, physical and interpretive, in the context of a game. The game is beautiful because the referee can be wrong, the result can be unfair, and some rules are suggestions of action enforced through interpretation.

Adding visual and computational media elements to games can diminish the importance of interpretation and negotiation as part of gameplay. VAR shows how depriving a game of the possibilities of interpretation and error does not make the game fairer, but rather a ghost of the pleasures it can afford to its players and spectators.

But there's a potential counterargument to this conservative view on using VAR in professional football. These lines were written in Spring 2025 in Barcelona. During that football season, a very young FC Barcelona, coached by Hansi Flick, used VAR to develop an exciting style of offensive play that depended on the accuracy of semi-automatic VAR. FC Barcelona would play with a very high defensive line, often positioned in the midfield, and move in perfect, choreographed synchronization. Usually, we would see an attacker running toward the goal and scoring against Barça, only for the goal to be disallowed because VAR showed that the attacker was offside, even if the referee had not initially seen the violation. Sometimes, these offsides were just centimeters, impossible for the human eye to detect.

Flick created a lightning-fast, exciting football team that relied on the accuracy of VAR to devise one of the most entertaining ways to play the game in Europe that season. Without technology, playing that way is not possible. It does not matter how well-trained the defensive line is; with the offside rule, there is always a possibility of error and interpretation. That was, as we argued, part of its beauty. However, Flick's 2024–2025 Barça showed how coaches and players can effectively adapt technology to enhance the beauty of play. If the offside rule becomes less interpretable, less prone to error, because of VAR, then let's play with the most aggressive offside trap possible, because players know that if there is offside, regardless of the outcome of play, the referee will have to take it into account.

Technology does not need to dictate how we act. Technology brings forth a set of affordances and politics to a particular human situation, in this case, game playing. We can, as players, either surrender to what the technology implicitly demands—namely, the elimination of human interpretation and rule-based ambiguity —or adapt technology and make it serve our ways of playing. When we play a game, we are not subject to technology. Technology should help us play, even if that means constantly exploring the edges of rules and technological constraints. That is, perhaps, the offside zone of the future of play.

STAYING ONSIDE

One of our ambitions with this book is to communicate how we, as game scholars, watch and understand football. We aim to share the vocabulary of game studies with those who love the game but want to understand it in a different context, alongside all the other games and sports. In this chapter, we examined the offside rule and presented how rules can contribute to the aesthetic beauty of a game. We introduced the idea by C. Thi Nguyen that games are the art of agency, and we examined how the offside rule not only modifies individual and collective agency but also the material conditions of the game, and how it requires human judgment to enforce the rule. We discussed the limits of VAR and other technical aids, and what these technological encroachments do to the aesthetics of games.

Game studies is a way of understanding games—learning why we care about them, what role they play in our lives, and how we create them. Understanding the elusive beauty of games and explaining why and how a game can become an aesthetic experience isn't something that can be summarized in a single chapter. What we want to do here is different from the usual. We don't look at the beauty of football through athleticism or skills, but through the game's structure. If there's one thing we've learned from the data revolution in sports, it's that there are underlying patterns of action that people tend to appreciate. In this chapter, we connect those patterns—not just the offside defense and the attacker's skills—but to a rule. By doing this, we hope to add a new layer to how we view the game of football.

And, perhaps more importantly, a new critical perspective that allows us to better evaluate when and how rules and their enforcement are being changed in the game. We have provided an argument explaining why VAR simplifies the aesthetics of the game and, consequently, influences the appeal of football. By viewing rules as contributing to the beauty of the game, we now have a broader vocabulary to argue that, even if minor, any modifications to the game can affect the fragile and fleeting beauty of the most beautiful game.

NOTES

1 Pippo Inzaghi top 10 Champions League goals. YouTube. www.youtube.com/watch?v=YU-MYJwUr3E&t=80s
2 Nguyen, 2020.
3 Best, 1988.
4 Sharp, 2015.
5 Elcombe, 2012.
6 Critchley, 2017.
7 Tavinor, 2009.
8 Let us sneak a defense of football in this endnote, one that may be more passional than academic. Football is an entertaining, beautiful game, precisely because it is a low-scoring game. All actions matter in football. The rarity of goals is not a defect and is fundamental to understanding how the game is played, thought, and experienced. It is a game of moments, a game of errors, a game of memorable instances that take time to build. Maybe other sports such as basketball are closer to performance art, like dances. Football, at its best, is a durational art.
9 The literature on VAR and the offside rule is already quite extensive. See Bordner, 2015; Chen and Davidson, 2022; Fasold et al., 2019; Hüttermann et al., 2017; Mather, 2020.
10 A good article on the notion of fairness in VAR is Svantesson, 2014.
11 This article explores a critical approach to the application of VAR: Pitt, 2021.
12 See Collins, 2010; Panse and Mahabaleshwarkar, 2020.
13 Mather, 2020.
14 See Aragão e Pina et al., 2018; Bordner, 2015; Boyer et al., 2020; Fasold et al., 2019; Maruenda, 2004.

CHAPTER 3

Can Football Be Automated?

Data, Intelligence, and Play

Moments of beauty in sports are brief and fleeting, yet they hold power in our memory because they define the sport. Basketball fans will never forget Dr. J's beautiful flight behind the backboard. Greg Louganis gracefully defied gravity with his jumps in the Barcelona Olympics. Serena and Venus Williams demonstrated the beauty of tennis in a unique point in Lexington in 2020 (Serena won). There are moments like these in football, too. But we are not going to write about them yet. We just want you to think about the beauty of sports, so we can talk about intelligence, human and artificial, and play.

This chapter will introduce why games are fascinating for artificial intelligence (AI) research. Games serve as excellent examples for understanding human intelligence. Following this, we will focus on the data revolution in football: the growing significance of computational modeling in shaping how the game is coached and played. We will present this data revolution as analogous to AI research in games: a quest for the nature of intelligence as expressed in gameplay. The chapter concludes with a reflection on the future of data in football and why the beauty of football may lie in its inherent elusiveness to AI.

DOI: 10.1201/9781003636762-4

Let's start with two moments of beauty in play, apparently unrelated yet fundamental to understanding games, sports, and intelligence. In the famous Go match between Lee Sedol and DeepMind's AlphaGo,[1] the result mattered: a machine beat for the first time a player in one of the most complex games designed by humans.[2] There was space for beauty in this high-stakes game that pitted the best of humans against the best of machines. In the second match, the machine performed a move that made no human sense but resulted in a beautiful victory for the computer. Move 37 was unique and beautiful. It can be explained in statistical terms, but that shortens its impact. For us in the audience, for other players, and for experts, there is no other way to understand Move 37 than by seeing its beauty. Move 37 was the Fosbury jump for machine learning and AI: a leap into the future of games and humanity.

What would be football's Move 37? Maybe Marco Van Basten's impossible volley to win the Euro Cup in 1988, or Maradona's cosmic goal in 1986 against England, dribbling around an empire. Perhaps Pelé's famous dummy against Uruguay, celebrated for not scoring a goal. Consider Brandi Chastain's penalty to win the 1999 World Cup—not the best penalty ever, but an iconic celebration that changed the game. Among many options, we chose a less well-known, more recent fleeting moment of football brilliance. It doesn't involve athleticism or a goal but rather a mastery of the game's essence. In the Euro 2020 match between Spain and Switzerland, Spanish midfielder Pedri receives the ball on the left side of the pitch, facing his own goal. Three Swiss players start to press: one closing down on Pedri, another cutting off his natural turn for his right foot, and another closing the passing lane to the defensive midfielder. With his first touch, Pedri passes the ball into the space between the advancing Swiss defenders, using their momentum to prevent interceptions and spark an attack. That first touch pass comes from the future: it considers not only where players are now but where they will be once the ball moves. In doing so speeds up the game and creates space where there was none.[3]

Football is a game of space and time, played with a ball. While athleticism is necessary in the modern game, football requires mental agility and spatial intelligence above all other skills. As Cruyff put it, "football is played with the head, and the legs are there to help".[4] Pedri's pass illustrates exactly that: a mastery of space and time performed by bodies, using a ball. That pass is pure football intelligence.

In this age of intelligent machines, the question is: can a computer develop football intelligence? Let's start with the apparent problem: football is a highly embodied sport. A robot won't be able to play football at a human level soon. And when it does, the fact that it can play football will be the least of our concerns. If we ever have robots that can play football with the intelligent athleticism of Wendy Renard or Zlatan Ibrahimovic. In that case, the least of our troubles should be whether they can play football.

This is not a science fiction book, so why should we write about automated football? Because it serves as an entry point to understanding why AI researchers find games fascinating.[5] Games provide the best environments for studying intelligence and the forms of intelligence machines can develop. Right now, a robot cannot score a bicycle kick like Zlatan Ibrahimovic. However, a computer can help identify the next Zlatan, assist English defender Lucy Bronze in recognizing patterns in her upcoming opponents attacking moves, and suggest how to counteract them. It can also discern logic in the chaos on the pitch that even the most experienced coaches may overlook.[6] While we are not yet close to machines that can outplay human football players, we are nearing the point *where* machines can *understand* the game of football as well as we do, if not better. We are closer to a Move 37 situation in football than we have ever been, and that provides a compelling reason to consider the impact thinking machines have on football and what football can teach us about AI.

UNDERSTANDING FOOTBALL INTELLIGENCE FOR HUMANS (AND MACHINES)

The beauty of Pedri's pass could be explained in a sentence: "a pass that breaks defensive pressure by reading the future positions of players and makes those future positions irrelevant". However, it could also be described in a more procedural manner: Pedri receives the ball with his back to the opposing team. He has noticed two players closing in on him while a third is closing fast on the most obvious passing lane. Right before receiving the ball, Pedri *calculates* that the best pass is the one that accounts for the forward momentum of the third defender so that the ball can reach a teammate. Pedri then uses the inside of his right foot to pass the ball with enough force and spin that it curls behind the forward-moving attacker.

This second description highlights the decision-making processes that Pedri underwent to perform that pass. This breakdown shows how football is a game of decisions made at speed to achieve a purpose, determined by the game's rules. The description also illustrates different forms of intelligence at play. And that is exactly why games are interesting for AI: they represent particular forms of intelligence within bounded environments where motives and actions are closely intertwined. Games are rule-based systems where most actions result from following rules toward a goal that is (usually) quantifiable and understandable. In other words: pass the ball, break the defense, run toward the goal, score. Do that in the most efficient way within the space created by the rules. Oh, and don't cheat.

In their foundational text on Artificial Intelligence,[7] Stuart Russell and Peter Norvig claim that "the abstract nature of games makes them an appealing subject for study. The state of a game is easy to represent, and agents are usually restricted to a small number of actions whose outcomes are defined by precise rules" (p. 161). Games are rule-based actions that occur within a constrained space and time, during which players agree to act according to clearly defined rules to achieve the predetermined goals they have assigned value to. A game scholar will recognize how Russell and Norvig's sentence translates the main arguments in Johan Huizinga's *Homo Ludens* into computer science. Huizinga claimed that play takes place separate from the world, in a context with its own rules that define the outcome and the players' actions. That is precisely why games are interesting for AI researchers.

There is a myth about the sportsperson as a relatively unintelligent individual whose only skills are to play within the rules of a sport, thanks to their superior physical abilities. However, the myth of the jock only demonstrates a limited understanding of the concept of intelligence. To excel in a sport, it is critical to utilize various forms of intelligence, from embodied to spatial and emotional. It is not trivial to be a jock.

Games should be viewed as exercises in intelligence. They follow clear rules that players must interpret while playing. Their goals are explicit and shared among participants. Games create and exist in worlds separate from, yet connected to, the uncertainties of the outside world. In the 2021 Olympics match between the US Women's National Team and Australia, Megan Rapinoe demonstrated a deep understanding of game rules. At 7:33 in the first half, she was preparing to take a corner kick. Corners are usually routine plays where the ball is aimed toward the area in hopes of a header. However, Rapinoe executed a creative and precise interpretation of the roles involved. A corner kick is a direct kick; meaning it can be used to attempt a shot on goal. Football is won by scoring goals. Seeing the Australian goalkeeper out of position, Rapinoe took her chance to score. And she did. This required intelligence to read the game situation, understanding the possibilities within the rules, and skill to curve the ball just enough so the goalkeeper couldn't block it. That wasn't just a goal scored from a corner—it was a display of football intelligence.[8]

Games are excellent probes to explore what human intelligence is and how machines can develop intelligence. Already at the birth of what we now understand as the field of AI research, the topic of games was addressed as central to understanding intelligence.[9]

AI researchers, however, are not particularly interested in physical games. They understand that the variability of play in these games and the role of embodied cognition in these physical games complicate exploring certain understandings of intelligence. Some games, such as chess or Go, are good benchmarks for logical, numerical, and a specific type of spatial intelligence. However, those are straightforward games, played on boards with few pieces that always behave consistently. While the combinatorics involved are mathematically impressive, they differ significantly from scoring a goal from the corner.

Before we continue, let's be clear: the biggest challenge in AI research is not developing intelligent machines, but understanding biological intelligence that translates into mechanical simulations of that unique characteristic. Some machines already behave "intelligently" in specific contexts: sorting out spam, correcting spelling mistakes, identifying handwriting, and playing chess. These forms of AI are localized, contextual, and functional; we understand sufficiently well what it means to be intelligent in that context to use a machine to perform those tasks intelligently.

Now think back to the football game, specifically to the vague idea of "the intelligent player". Everyone can see why Messi, Ronaldo, Marta, or Alexia Putellas are outstanding players at all levels. But what about quieter talents? While Alexia was the star of the FC Barcelona women's team that dominated Spain and Europe in 2020, the team wouldn't have functioned without the contributions of Aitana Bonmatí, the fearless, tireless player who kept that team moving from midfield with a mix of clever passing and movement. Claude Makelele was another one of these players: without his presence at the base of the midfield, a Real Madrid team with Ronaldo, Zidane, Figo, Beckham, and Roberto Carlos would have simply fallen apart, not just because of Makelele's work rate, but also because of his intelligence on the pitch.

If you're new to football, here's a good exercise: in that squad you love, find the invisible players who keep everything running smoothly. They might not be the most technically skilled, the most athletic, or the top scorers. But they are the players whose absence worsens their team's performance. All great squads include at least one of these players, and enjoying football begins with learning to recognize them.

What makes a player intelligent in football? Of course, the answer depends on their position on the pitch, but there are some general traits we can highlight: technical skills combined with a physique that supports them, whether through speed, strength, or a balance of both; an understanding of space and movement, both of the opponent and the team; a sense of timing with and without the ball; and an ability to assess the match situation—for example, why a 1-1 draw can be seen as the start of a victory or why a 2-0 lead can be the most dangerous lead.

Intelligence in football isn't just about a single trait. Being technically skilled, strong, agile, or fast isn't enough. Football intelligence comes from an embodied understanding of the game as it happens. Unlike games like chess or Go, where intelligence is about choosing the best strategy and moves based on the current board state, football requires multiple types of intelligence to work together simultaneously. In football, there aren't clear-cut states of the game, and there are few relevant, quantifiable, and computable markers of those states (there's score, time, and bookings, but not much more). In other words, there are very few actionable, computable data sources that a machine could use to perform the complex, interconnected decision-making needed to play the game at any level.

AI has become highly skilled at playing complex games like *Starcraft*, which can resemble football: multiple agents needing to coordinate to reach a goal while reacting in real time to changing conditions. However, the main difference is the amount of data generated by the game itself. Since it is a video game, a computer program has access to all the data being processed to shape the gameplay experience. While this is not trivial and highlights significant progress in understanding certain aspects of intelligence, bots beating humans at *Starcraft* is not only feasible but also predictable and expected. Therefore, even when we have an AI that surpasses humans at playing *FIFA*, we will still not be close to automating the game of football.

However, football can still be significant for AI. In the words of world-leading AI researcher Julian Togelius, "games are the future of AI. Games provide the best benchmarks for AI because of the way they are designed to challenge many different human cognitive abilities, as well as for their technical convenience and the availability of human data". The challenge here is not whether football can or will be automated, but how automation changes the game of football. Football demonstrates modalities of intelligence that could then be simulated by computers. As Togelius explains, "by studying how humans play and design games, we can understand how they think, and we can attempt to replicate this thinking by creating game-playing and game-designing AI agents". The challenge, then, is not how to automate football but how to capture what makes football a unique game in ways that are computable.

The answer to that challenge: a data revolution in football.

MONEYBALL AND THE BEAUTIFUL GAME

The goal of all modern professional sports is to achieve success both on the field and in financial profit. Sports organizations are no longer just community representatives but have become corporations where the main stakeholders are not those whose loyalty has been handed down through generations. We will examine the capitalist platformization of football later in this book, but it's important to mention now because football teams are competing in the Champions League and also ranking on the *Forbes* and *Fortune* lists; thus, gaining any competitive advantage is crucial to the corporate culture of sports. This underlines the importance of data-driven decision-making in sports management.

Michael Lewis' book *Moneyball: The Art of Winning an Unfair Game*, adapted for the big screen by Bennett Miller, Steven Zaillian, and Aaron Sorkin, provided the shorthand term for using data to increase a team's chances of success. The book's story goes as follows: baseball manager Billy Beane recruited data analyst Peter Brand, whose "sabermetric" method allowed for recruiting players based on data rather than good old-fashioned scouting. This recruitment policy resulted in a cheap and highly competitive team, forever changing sports scouting and analysis.

In football, data-driven decisions are a staple for most teams, with the Premier League hosting some of the most advanced data research units in any sport. In Denmark, FC Midtjylland became a sensation when it emerged as a competitive force in the local league, thanks to a data-driven approach to recruitment. Even FC Barcelona, the team that flourished in the late 20th Century thanks to the visionary competitive aesthetics of

Johan Cruyff, uses data to scout, recruit, and manage players from the academy to the first team.

But what is this data revolution, and why is it relevant in the context of AI and games?

So far in this chapter, we've explained that football cannot be automated (yet?) because many aspects of it cannot be modeled for computers to learn how to play the game. However, the difficulty of modeling football is not an obstacle but a challenge. Data scientists in football are developing computational models of the actions that occur on the pitch, enabling them to apply software tools to various phases of the game.[10] This is not the automation of football but a computational approach to enhancing our understanding of the game and improving it through human–AI collaboration. Data-driven football allows us to see the invisible—the patterns that emerge through time and space on the pitch. The data revolution enables us to view football from the perspective of algorithms, revealing aspects of the game that were previously unseen. Again, the focus of AI and data science is both the creation of "intelligent machines" and the understanding of what intelligence is. Data in football helps us understand what football intelligence is.

As an introductory example, let's discuss Expected Goals (xG). Initially developed by Sarah Hilditch and Vic Barnett,[11] xG is a statistical evaluation of the likelihood of scoring from a given chance. The statistic connects the placement of a shot on the pitch to the probability of a goal being scored.[12] If the shot is from outside the box, it's unlikely that it will result in a goal, so its xG is quite low. In contrast, if the shot originates within the box, the probability of scoring increases significantly. xG assists coaches in developing tactics to position their best players where their shots have a higher statistical chance of resulting in a goal. This represents human football intelligence enhanced by computational intelligence.[13]

xG gives a numeric value to the quality of a chance. Throughout this book, we're presenting a theme of the freedom of the game versus the push to make it predictable. xG reflects a novel attempt to try to understand aspects of the variability of the game to make it more predictable. It uses historical data to assess the quality of a shot. That statistical estimate can be aggregated to give a team an idea of how well they create chances. Teams can then develop tactics to make chances quantifiably better. This is acting on computable data to change gameplay, a form of human–machine collaboration that yields excellent results on the pitch. Football, then, *can* be automated.

How can game studies help make sense of football's data revolution? This question can only be answered by the part of game studies that analyzes digital games. Not for technological fetishism, but because of what data does to football. The data revolution results from using computational technologies to evaluate the computable elements of the game of football. In other words, it is learning to see football like a computer, perhaps even like some form of *computer game.*

Digital adaptations of games already serve this purpose. For instance, chess as a video game is a computational version of the traditional game of chess. Playing chess mainly involves calculations. There is little physical effort needed, as the game revolves around the 64-square board and the limited, predefined movements of each piece. Programming a computer to learn to play chess is a complex computer science challenge, but it is still easier than football because chess has clear rules, boundaries, and processes to reach goals.

That is the first challenge of automating football: its incredible variability. Consider a creative player like Megan Rapinoe. Her greatness is not just based on her skills or tactical discipline; she also has the ability to break expectations and regularly perform against the odds. Maybe this is what great football players are: those who can consistently produce statistical anomalies, making these anomalies feel normal.

In football, each player's movement and the playing field are continuous, not discrete units. This complexity makes computations more difficult. The challenge of the data revolutionaries is to learn how to see the game of football as a computing machine would. In the book *Footballmatics*, mathematician David Sumpter explains that "the challenge is finding a relatively small number of fundamental states of play, and working out how likely a team is to score or concede a goal from each of these states" (p. 287). If football ever becomes automated, it will result from this process of formalization of its structures so that the game becomes computable. This may prove impossible, but it is at the core of the data revolution. And like the applications of AI in games, using data to understand football provides insights into human intelligence, both on and off the pitch.

Despite all the challenges, elements of football have become computable. In doing so, we have learned novel ways to watch, coach, and play football. Sumpter explains the mathematical analysis of defending and optimal strategies. He highlights the work of Selina Pan and her group, who modeled defensive tactics to understand better how to close down space. In her modeled work,

> *beating the computerised defenders is impossible in theory as well as practice. Selina and her colleagues went on to give a mathematical proof that their zone-minimizing algorithm always wins. Unless the attacker is closer to a point on the line he is trying to get to (in this case, the edge of the box), then the defenders always catch the attacker. This explains why forwards such as Cristiano Ronaldo, Neymar, and Lyuis Suarez are so much more revered than defenders like Badstuber. While defenders may well be great artists, when forwards go past them, they are achieving the impossible.*
>
> *(pp. 63–64)*

This computational insight lets us recognize patterns of behavior in existing data. This recognition enables predictions that can be used on the pitch in real-time tactics and to inform coaching drills. Football is far from being fully understood computationally, like Go or Chess, but we are closer to understanding some of its aspects through data. In doing so, we gain a deeper understanding of the game. What made great defenders *great*? Baresi, Hierro, Puyol, Irene Paredes, and Wendy Renard all share the ability to close down space, reducing the options available to attackers. Those of us who love the game had an instinct about this, but thanks to the data revolution, we can now explain it and even identify it in other players to help coach them toward those skills—even when innate talent doesn't carry them that far. The game may not be automated, but it's gradually becoming more *data-driven*.

With this in mind, let's return to the xG metric and examine its impact on the game. When German coach Thomas Tuchel took over the English club Chelsea, he introduced not only one of the most innovative approaches to tactics and positional play but also a focus on metrics and their application on the pitch. In the 2020–2021 season, Tuchel's Chelsea made a successful run in the Champions League by basing their play on the constant movement of the forward players, intense pressure, and a few but high-quality chances. Utilizing xG as a metric to support his tactics, Tuchel aimed for his team to shoot less but with greater precision. When your players include the likes of Mason Mount or Kai Havertz, enhancing the quality of their chances leads to more goals, even if they shoot at goal less often.

Typically, we expect attacking teams to shoot frequently because the basic logic of the game says that if you don't shoot, you don't score. However, this isn't always true when shooting means sacrificing better scoring chances. Taking many shots from outside the box may look impressive from the stands, but it is actually a less smart strategy than creating attacking patterns that allow you to take fewer shots from inside the box. What looks impressive on TV or from the stands isn't always the smartest approach to the game. This tradeoff was hidden until xG provided coaches and analysts with a tool to *identify* what really makes a good scoring chance in football. Once again, data shows its value by revealing patterns that were previously invisible, which can then be coached to improve performance.

THE SEARCH FOR FOOTBALL'S MOVE 37

This chapter begins by reflecting on the famous Move 37 in the AlphaGo—Lee Sedol duel. Move 37 serves as a guiding light for researchers interested in the automation of games and sports: when we enable a machine to create unexpected and inhuman moves, we will achieve true game-playing AI. The search for football's Move 37 is underway, utilizing data approaches that reveal hidden patterns at play in football.

Football won't be automated anytime soon. Still, the growing role of computational methods in analyzing, training, and evaluating gameplay raises questions about what automation in a game really means and what effects these methods have on game development. The ongoing question remains: what is the data-driven future of football?

At the time of writing this chapter, the 2022 World Cup—a highly controversial event—is coming to an end. An event that should never have taken place in a country unfit to host such tournaments, the 2022 World Cup may be remembered as a turning point for FIFA's corruption during an era of sportswashing. At the same time, it will also be remembered for marking Germany's third consecutive elimination in the group stage. While this is remarkable in itself, it becomes even more interesting considering that Germany recorded the most xG per match in their group. Is this an example of data being blind? Or, as conservative pundits would put it, a limit to what data reveals about "the soul of the game"?

The answer is neither. Germany was great at creating good chances, but those chances still need to be turned into goals. That's what makes football a sport: transforming opportunities into goals is so difficult that it defines the game as a low-scoring, high-stakes competition. Data-driven approaches to analyzing and coaching football do not make the game easy to compute, like Go or Chess. The difficulty of automating football is exactly what makes it so unique: even with accurate models that describe and predict actions, football remains too unpredictable and chaotic to be easily automated. Nonetheless, data-driven approaches to football are here to stay, and we need to consider their potential effects on the game.

What does it take for something to be automatable? The first step is to translate it into a form that a computing machine can perform operations with: binary data structured as information that can be computed. The process of translating an analog reality into a numeric representation, by definition, changes its nature; it may occasionally flatten it to whatever can be computed.

When people who love football complain about the growing importance of data in the professional game, their argument often follows these lines: the game loses its soul, and computers cannot and will never be able to appreciate the intangible qualities of the game. This critique actually has a foundation of truth: all models are wrong, but some of them are useful. Translating football into computational models flattens the game; it turns athletic beauty into something quite different. Think about this paragraph from the book *Football Hackers*:[14]

> *A defender playing the ball past two strikers into midfield increases the goalscoring probability by an average rate of 0.5 per cent. If his pass is received in front of the opposition back four, the probability goes up by nearly 5 per cent. The cumulative effect of these actions over the course of 90 minutes can be surmised in one value. If it's 0.2, it stands for a player adding 20 per cent to the probability of a goal being scored.*
>
> *(p. 224)*

This model of football behavior offers phenomenal insight into what makes a good defender in the modern game of playing from the back. At the same time, does this paragraph truly convey the greatness of Mapi León or Franz Beckenbauer? What is lost when we reduce complex human agency to a numeric representation?

Shoshanna Zuboff, the scholar known for defining "surveillance capitalism", coined another useful term in her study of organizations: informating.[15] Organizations often engage in processes that quantify activities and operations through systems that make these activities visible to the organization itself. For example, consider software that tracks work hours or monitors sales performance. The difference between analog and digital systems of *informating* is that software generates new streams of information that are utilized to gain insights about the organization, potentially leading to new processes. Informating is a phenomenon with both positive and negative aspects. Positively, it promotes the recognition and acknowledgment of various types of labor within organizations and can be used to develop more efficient and creative ways of engaging with work. Negatively, it can act as a tool of control and may lead to a flattening of activities: creativity, invention, and innovation are difficult to capture through informating tools, and therefore, they are often lost in this process. What cannot be computed ceases to exist, ceases to be relevant, and as a result, all automated work ends up being bland repetitions of what is already being done. Creativity and nonconformist solutions die out with informating.

A pessimist might say that modern football is undergoing a process of data-driven change. The data revolution enables coaches, analysts, and players to better understand what happens on and off the pitch, and it introduces new ways of thinking about creativity, competition, and talent. Much of the work that data analysts do for football actually contributes to the positive effects of this data-driven change, such as helping players reach their potential and developing tactical solutions that more effectively achieve goals. Tuchel's focus on creating quality chances rather than numerous chances led Chelsea to display a remarkably beautiful, highly dynamic, almost choreographed attacking style where no players had fixed positions, and all moved into space in search of the right shot.

However, the data revolution could also lead to a certain flattening of the game. Keep in mind, this is not happening yet, and it probably won't, but, like all informating processes, it's important to issue a warning. Informating relies on specific technology to observe a phenomenon. That technology comes with a worldview: for a phenomenon to be recognized by the data, it needs a model, a hypothesis, and a data source. Since all data is historical, most predictions are based on past data, risking the game becoming limited to repeating patterns from the past, which results in nothing new. Would our data models today be able to capture the greatness of Marta, Johann Cruyff, and Maradona, who were all outliers when it comes to the standards of what a football player should be?

Again, most data analysts are aware of this problem, and it is unlikely that this flattening of the game will happen, mainly because there is too much enjoyable chaos in football for it to become a mechanical game like chess. However, as with all processes of informating, we should always consider what perspectives we use to analyze the data, and what becomes invisible when applying a specific model to describe the world. What might be overlooked is the quiet brilliance of a player or the mysterious creativity of another.

INTELLIGENCE AND FOOTBALL

This chapter begins by questioning whether football can be automated. Our response evolved into a comprehensive reflection on data, software, and intelligence. This is also where we will conclude the chapter.

In *Playing Smart*, Togelius asks the reader to evaluate what they do when they are playing a game, whether digital or analog:

> *let's look at what you are really doing:* You plan (...), You think spatially (...), You predict the game and your opponent(s) (...) You assess yourself (...) you move (...) In sum, we use many different forms of intelligence when we play games, more or less all the time.
>
> *(pp. 13–19)*

Playing games is an act of intelligence, and playing games intelligently is a feat often celebrated in our culture. Games are prisms through which we see the many manifestations of intelligence in humans and across species and artificial forms of agency.

Games are valuable tools for understanding AI, and using AI in (digital) games has led to major advances in game design and our understanding of intelligence. Since football is a game, it's logical to ask whether it can be automated and what lessons we can learn from that.

To be honest, the question of automation is irrelevant. What truly matters is what football *as a sport* reveals about human and AI. Whether AI can play football better than humans is actually a secondary concern to why football highlights various forms of human intelligence and what we can learn from that display to apply in AI.

The data revolution in football aims to use computational systems and models to reflect the complex nature of human intelligence displayed on the field. Capturing details like spatial movement, pass accuracy, the balance between teamwork and individual skill, and the intangible qualities that make football the beautiful game is a major challenge. The goal of data and AI in football should not be to automate the sport. Instead, it should focus on developing tools that enhance and celebrate human intelligence on the field. While football cannot be fully automated, integrating machine intelligence and generating new insights to reveal unseen aspects can make the game more engaging, creative, and intelligent.

NOTES

1 The Lee Sedol versus Alpha Go match has been the subject of many accounts in science and journalism. We find this write-up by Wired to be the most approachable text on the event: www.wired.com/2016/03/two-moves-alphago-lee-sedol-redefined-future/ (accessed 12/5/2025). The 2017 documentary by Greg Kohs is another relevant source for becoming familiar with the importance of this event: www.imdb.com/title/tt6700846/ (accessed 12/5/2025).
2 See Silver et al., 2016, 2017.
3 We are not the only fans of this pass: see an account of it here: https://tribuna.com/en/news/fcbarcelona-2021-07-02-how-did-he-even-see-that-pedri-pulls-off-mindblowing-pass-vs-switzerland/
4 We source the quote from this article written on the event of Cruyff's passing: www.theguardian.com/football/2016/mar/24/you-play-football-with-your-head-and-your-legs-are-there-to-help-you-johan-cruyff-in-quotes (accessed 12/5/2025).
5 See Togelius, 2019; Yannakakis and Togelius, 2018.
6 Good overviews of the importance of data analytics in modern football can be read in Sumpter, 2016; Biermann, 2019; Link, 2018; Rein and Memmert, 2016.
7 Russell and Norvig, 2021.
8 A video of the goal can be found here: www.youtube.com/watch?v=SwZjkVIxbys.
9 The foundational text on artificial intelligence is Turing, 1950.
10 See Pu et al., 2024; Geppert et al., 2022.
11 Barnett and Hilditch, 1993.
12 Mead, O'Hare, and McMenemy, 2023; Ensum, Pollard, and Taylor, 2004.
13 A good visual explanation of what Expected Goals is and how it looks like can be found here: https://theanalyst.com/articles/what-is-expected-goals-xg.
14 Biermann, 2019.
15 Zuboff, 1988.

CHAPTER 4

Possibility Space

A SPORT LIKE FOOTBALL IS learned both by watching and playing. The latter forces us to discover the limits of our bodies: our hand-eye coordination, running ability, and skills in directing a ball with our feet when kicking. Watching football is also a learning process; it teaches us not only to look at the ball but also at the space where the game is played.

This chapter explores how game design theory can enhance our understanding of football. It also introduces game design terminology to help grasp the data revolution in football and its potential to raise this respected sport alongside video games and other digital entertainment forms. Additionally, this chapter discusses the idea of greatness in football. Like all sports, football involves debates over who the greatest players and coaches are. By understanding how game designers create games, we provide another perspective for recognizing and explaining greatness in the beautiful game.

Before we start, a quick note: this chapter only introduces basic game design ideas and literature. Over the past 30 years, game design scholarship has grown into a fairly mature field that explains how games are made, the terminology and methods designers use to create engaging experiences

DOI: 10.1201/9781003636762-5

across different media, from software to cardboard. In this sense, this chapter is just a brief introduction to game design. We will suggest literature and resources that can deepen a curious reader's understanding. Still, our main focus will be on a core game design concept and how it applies to analyzing football.

That concept is known as the "possibility space", sometimes called the "state space". We will draw on two primary game studies references: Katie Salen and Eric Zimmerman's classic *Rules of Play*, and Robert Zubek's more recent *Elements of Game Design*.[1] These two texts provide a comprehensive definition of this concept, focused on its applicability as both a design tool and an analytic lens to understand how games are played.

Designing games is challenging. After all, a game is a technology created to generate entertainment and fun. As a field, it sits at the intersection of psychology, philosophy, design research, material studies, and many other areas. Game designers shape experiences by restricting our actions in ways that let us enjoy ourselves without feeling too confined by those artificial limits. They build worlds, define ways of existing within those worlds, and then let players explore and find joy. In this chapter, we will look at how game design can teach us to observe, analyze, and create the different kinds of fun that football brings.

A GAME DESIGN PRIMER

A game is a set of rules that restrict players' actions, allowing them to reach a goal they care about in ways they find enjoyably challenging. There are many other definitions of games, and the field of game studies often has endless debates about what makes a game. We will not get into that here, as our aim is to use game design to understand the game of football. This simple definition of a game works well for our purposes.

The first key aspect of this definition is that games involve rules that restrict human actions in a way that is both enjoyable and engaging. In football, these rules are collectively known as The Laws of the Game and are overseen by the International Football Association Board (IFAB). The official rules are available on the IFAB's website and are regularly updated after each board meeting.

Football is a team-based invasion game.[2] The rules stipulate that two teams must invade the opposing team's side of the pitch to score a goal in a designated area. They must advance the ball into the opponent's territory using only their feet to accomplish this. The goal of this invasion is for the ball to enter a specific area of the pitch, known as the goal, which a player with special abilities protects: the ability to use their hands. The rules also outline the game's duration, the pitch's size, and other elements that define football as we know it. Reviewing the rules shows that football is enjoyable because it involves numerous regulations that complicate the ball's movement from one side of the pitch to the other. The most important rule is that the ball can only be advanced using feet.

Football is the outcome of rule changes over time, as Jonathan Wilson details in the classic *Inverting the Pyramid.*[3] Still, we're more interested in *how* the game is designed rather than its history. Like all games, football is intentionally designed. Game design involves a process that uses various methods to create, evaluate, and regulate rule sets, spaces, and materials, all aimed at generating enjoyable experiences. From a design perspective, games are technologies created for play. Game design is the discipline that develops and assesses the methods used to make games.

Before we continue discussing game design, we want to make a quick comment about "sports". We don't want to conflict with academic disciplines, fields, and personalities. For the rest of this chapter, we assume that a sport is a game that includes several social and material practices that evolve together and often involve some form of embodied challenge. We propose that sports are games played with and for your body. Thus, all sports are games, but not all games are sports. As a discipline, game design draws from psychology, philosophy, engineering, and mathematics to create enjoyable experiences by limiting what people can do and encouraging them to accept those limitations willingly.

Essentially, game design establishes rules, environments, and props that facilitate enjoyable experiences for players. It creates a setting and an opportunity for people to engage in rule-based actions, with the promise of fun. Designing games differs from designing can openers or loudspeakers, where form must follow function and tasks should be completed efficiently. Unlike many other types of design, game design fails if it too narrowly dictates what players can do. Game design is similar to architecture in that it sets a context, provides rules, and allows players to discover enjoyment while carefully guiding them through the experience. For example, in football, the laws of the game do not specify which part of the foot should be used to kick the ball, as that would diminish the enjoyment. The rules also do not dictate the formations or tactics of each team, an important point we will revisit later in the chapter and in throughout the rest of the book. The Laws of the Game create a framework within which players, willingly accepting the limitation of hitting the ball only with their feet, can find ways to have fun. In this sense, game design is "second-order design": it does not create an object but a situation where users will find the best ways to address their needs.

Designing involves working with materials to create forms that fulfill specific needs. Metal, plastic, wood, and cloth are all classic materials in design. However, what constitutes the material of *game* design? While an intuitive answer might lead us to the same types of materials mentioned earlier, we prefer a more creative approach. The actual material of game design is people. Game designers primarily engage with individuals' emotional, cognitive, and physical capacities. Since game design is second-order, ultimately shaped by the players who will *interact with* the game, designers must understand player psychology, including emotions, logic, and morality, to determine what is enjoyable for them and how to create it.

For example, some players find it fun to accumulate items that have been assigned value and are artificially scarce, which leads to *Monopoly*. For others, fun comes from the freedom to create a different personality and experience life through it, as seen in *Dungeons and Dragons*. For football players, fun is the tangible pleasure of overcoming the challenge of controlling a ball with their feet while attempting to score a goal with their teammates against an opposing team. It's a game that showcases skill by presenting it as a competition.

To work with this material, game designers create rules that constrain player actions while providing specific tools to solve the artificially created problems. These tools are often called "game mechanics"[4] and can be understood as the verbs players use while playing the game. In football, these mechanics include passing, shooting, throwing, tackling, and others. These mechanics are matched with challenges defined by rules, such as being unable to use your hands, creating the offside position, or forbidding goalkeepers from using their feet when a player from their team passes the ball. All these constraints and possibilities shape the game's world, where players voluntarily enter, interact with each other, and adapt the game to have fun in their own way, whether by following or breaking the rules.

Game design research has developed a comprehensive vocabulary that describes the processes of translating types of fun into game mechanics and rules that players engage with. By placing players at the center of the design process and recognizing that game design serves as a setting for player action, game developers are becoming more fluent in the interdisciplinary understandings necessary to comprehend player experiences as mediated by a game.

The concept we will draw from game design is the possibility space, which describes how game designers see the world and how their understanding of game development and knowledge can be applied to football. Game design knowledge helps understand football because it is also a carefully planned game. As we mentioned earlier, the laws of the game are updated by the IFAB, an organization with several technical committees responsible for evaluating changes in game rules.

In the video game industry, notable game designers include John Romero, creator of the classic *Doom*, and Danielle Bunten Berry, a programmer and designer of *M.U.L.E.*, an early and highly influential multiplayer video game. In the world of board games, German designer Reiner Knizia is as close to a star as the genre has, with Klaus Teuber of *Catan* fame perhaps being the closest it gets to a household name. But what about football? Who are the star game designers of the sport? While many former players, coaches, referees, and academics have left their mark on the game, we suggest Arsene Wenger as the equivalent of John Romero in football. As a coach, Wenger revolutionized the Premier League by introducing science-based methods, nutritional research, and innovative tactical approaches to Arsenal, leading to a legendary team that finished unbeaten in the 2003–2004 season. After retiring from active coaching, Wenger became FIFA's Chief of Global Football Development. This role gave him control and influence over the evolution of football, from video assistant refereeing (VAR) to advances in athleticism and player training.

We want to highlight Wenger as a game designer to emphasize that football, like all games, is developed through iterative processes to create enjoyable experiences for both players and spectators. The concept of the possibility space helps us frame some of the work that football designers do. It also allows us to understand different aspects of coaching, the purpose of specific training drills, and development techniques. Additionally, it offers a framework for explaining ideas of "greatness" in football and the extraordinary events that can happen on a football pitch. Ultimately, our goal is to show how game design theory can be a valuable tool for understanding the beautiful game.

MAPPING POSSIBILITY SPACES

Learning to play a game is not an easy task. For some people, it comes naturally, but for most of us, navigating the rules and developing the right skills to overcome challenges takes time. In their classic game design textbook, *A Game Design Vocabulary*,[5] Naomi Clark and Anna Anthropy explain how we learn to play *Super Mario Bros* by simply playing the first level, a game tutorial. In *Super Mario*, the first thing we see is our avatar, Mario, placed centrally on the screen. We try to walk right and left and soon realize that we must walk right to access the rest of the level. Soon, we encounter some enticing blocks marked with a "?". This teaches us to jump, hit them, and earn a reward. We are then introduced to enemies, which we learn to avoid, but we can also jump on top of them to eliminate them. The level then progresses by combining those few possible actions (move, jump, collect) until we reach the end, marked with a flag.

Without any instructions or guidance for the player, *Super Mario* has shown us how to play the game. In fact, nearly all modern video games have dedicated tutorials that teach players the rules, the main actions they can perform, and how those actions affect their progress toward the goal. These tutorials also explain why the game is fun and what skills are needed to play. Even some board games include something similar to a tutorial, often through simplified scenarios and rules to help players learn, like *Magic Maze*, or detailed descriptions of gameplay sequences in the manual that clarify the finer points of an action, such as in *Pandemic*.[6]

Tutorials are fundamental to a game's success because they explain how to play. In game design terms, tutorials present players with a space of possibility. Good tutorials give players a glimpse of the game's world, what they can and cannot do, and how to do it. In doing so, they shape a mental model that game players use to learn how to play. This mental model represents the space of possibility.

Think about it: when we start playing a game, before we know all the rules, maybe all actions are possible.[7] We know there are rules that we need to adhere to and learn to navigate these constraints using the tools that designers have given us. The combination of the game's rules and the actions afforded to the player to achieve the goals they can formulate at a particular point defines the space of possibility in a game. This space of possibility evolves through gameplay, changing as the rules change and as the player's skills to see, understand, and pursue new goals evolve.

In *Tic-Tac-Toe*, for example, the possibility space at the beginning of the game is quite ample. We know we must place a circle or a cross in the 3 × 3 grid. The number of different starting positions in that game is 27. The possibilities decrease once the first item is placed until none are left. Because the space of possibility in *Tic-Tac-Toe* is so limited, the game tends to be rather dull.

In many sequential games, it is possible to formulate the possibility space mathematically. Games like *Chess* or *Go* have astronomically large possibility spaces.[8] These vast spaces of possibility make the games challenging, strategically deep, and the perfect target for the assumption that intelligence equals the ability to make decisions to navigate these possibility spaces. This is why artificial intelligence researchers have focused considerable effort on teaching computers to play these games better than humans, as their premise was that the capacity to traverse large possibility spaces equates to intelligence[9]. However, making the right choices to select the most favorable actions to achieve the goals we set for ourselves reflects a particular form of intelligence, one tied to computability and limited, sequential, rule-based activities. But what about a game like Super Mario Bros? The action isn't sequential; there are no clear steps, and the environment constantly changes based on the players' actions, without turns. Yet, we have achieved immense success in teaching machines to play Super Mario Bros on their own. We did this by training machines to perceive potential actions as they emerge in smaller time frames. In other words, we've learned how to turn Super Mario Bros, a game with continuous actions, into a game where an artificial agent can perceive a structured space of possibilities every few steps. The computer figures out what to do within that space, moves to the next step, evaluates it, acts, and then continues. Although the game progresses continuously, the artificial agent is trained to see it as a series of perceived possibility spaces. After all, this is similar to how we play video games: we assess our situation and decide what to do based on that assessment.

This explains how game design theory suggests two different versions of the concept of the space of possibility. There is the *formal* space of possibility, an ideal defined by all the actions that could be taken legally within the rules. And then there's the perceived space of possibility, which is the actions a player considers possible and doable at a given time. The *formal* space of possibility is much larger than the perceived space of possibility. The *perceived* space of possibility expands as players learn to play the game, develop skills, and thus allow designers to introduce new challenges.

A game designer's main tasks are to create a *formal* space of possibility that contains many different potentials for the evolution of play toward a particular type of fun, and to shape the various *perceived* spaces of possibility that players engage with as they play the game. Tutorials present one space of possibility. Each level introduces new possibilities that players may or may not *perceive* depending on their skill level, interests, and personal goals. Ultimately, players are the ones who decide what space of possibility they perceive. Most of us see the game as designers nudge us to see, but others see *more* of the game. Speedrunners know the possibility of achieving goals faster than anybody else by recognizing the boundaries and limits of the game.[10] Cheaters see a space of possibility that expands when breaking the rules. Creative players view the space of possibility not as an instruction set, but as a canvas for expression. In the end, the efforts of game designers focus on ensuring that players perceive fun possibilities, but they cannot determine that all players will inhabit those spaces, as they may create their own.

LEARNING SPACES

So, how does all of this relate to football? Football is a continuous game, more similar to *Super Mario Bros* than to *Chess*. The IFAB defines the formal space of possibility for the game. But what makes football special is the perceived space of possibility, as that is where the beauty, pleasure, and importance of football reside. To map these perceptions, let's explore how children learn to play the game, based on the Danish standards for youth training, while also reflecting on some classics in the field.

In Denmark, football training is divided into different age groups, each with its own method for organizing matches and teams. In the first stage, players aged 4 to 7 (U4 to U7) use a field measuring 21 × 13 meters, where the game is played with teams of three players and goals that are 1 × 1.5

meters. In the second stage, from U8 to U10, matches are held on a field measuring 30 × 40 meters, with teams of five players and goals sized 1.5 × 3.0 meters. In the final stage of children's football, from U11 to U13, the fields are 68 × 52.5 meters, goals are 5 × 2 meters, and teams consist of eight players. From U14 onward, players are trained to play 11-a-side with standard rules, including the offside rule (see Figure 4.1).

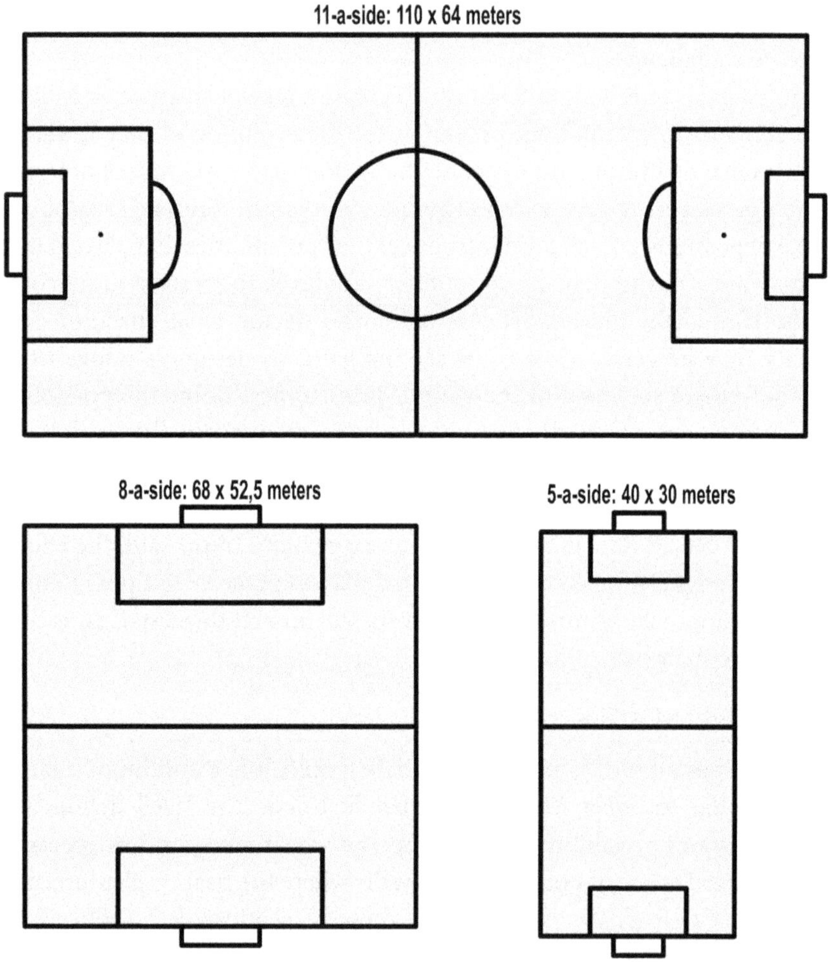

FIGURE 4.1 Different pitch sizes, from development to professional stages.

There are many pedagogical reasons behind the different sizes of pitches and goals, but most relate to one fundamental skill football players need to develop: the ability to perceive evolving possibilities in the game. Because football is a continuous sport, the space of possibilities for each player changes as the game unfolds. At every moment, a player faces numerous options for their actions. This is a large but finite number, depending on many factors, including who has possession of the ball and a player's individual skills. To help players develop the skill of perceiving how available choices emerge from a space of possibility, football training begins by limiting the number of players, roles, and the size of the pitch and goal.

In 3v3, there are fewer possible spaces, giving players more time to recognize and respond to them. As they develop this skill, players move on to more complex versions of the game where the available spaces and options increase accordingly. To learn to play football, players go through iterations of the game that offer limited choices and spaces, helping them align their perception of possibilities with their actions and the game situation. In other words, learning to play football involves recognizing all the available possibilities during play and making appropriate decisions based on those options.

In fact, a key aspect of training exercises is to help players improve their ability to make correct decisions under pressure. Technique and physical fitness are important parts of training. However, a large part of modern football training focuses on developing decision-making skills, tactical understanding, and physical ability to recognize what can and should be done at any moment on the field. The Austrian coach and educator Horst Wein is one of the most influential figures in 20th-century football education. His work, which has significantly influenced the training methods of successful clubs like FC Barcelona, is based on the idea that effective football training happens with the ball through simulations of match situations. The goal is not to create robotic responses to those situations, but to teach players to make the right decisions by recognizing the options available to them, whether they have possession or are defending.

Two of his most well-known training drills illustrate this concept. The rondo, also called "piggy in the middle", is a simple activity where players form a circle, with one or two players in the center. The aim is for the players in the circle to pass the ball to each other without losing possession. The two players in the middle try to block the passes. If a pass is broken up or of poor quality, the player who loses the ball moves to the middle, and a chaser takes their place. This basic drill combines passing technique with decision-making under pressure. A player in the circle must be ready to receive the ball, quickly evaluate the position of the chasers, and decide whom to pass to. Meanwhile, a chaser must read the situation: where the intended receiver is and how to intercept the pass. Rondo helps players develop the ability to perceive passing options within the circle and act accordingly, whether to make a good pass or apply effective pressure. Through this drill, players improve their decision-making skills in both passing and defense by exploring overlapping areas of possibility (see Figure 4.2).

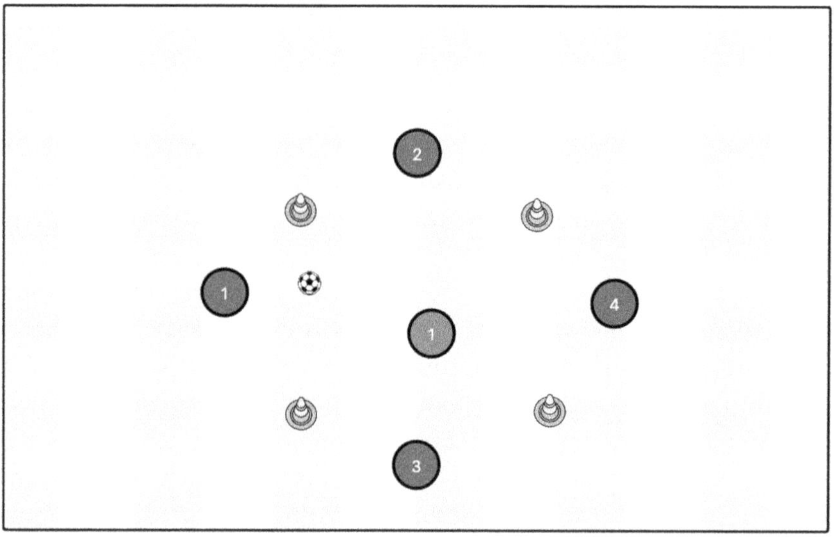

FIGURE 4.2 The rondo exercise.

Another classic drill is a soccer game on a small field, where each team defends two small goals instead of one large goal. In other words, each team has two physical goals rather than one. There are no goalkeepers in this drill, and the field is usually short and wide. A team can score in either of the opponent's goals. The goal of this drill is to teach players to use the entire width of the field and to move the ball side to side while searching for an open goal. This drill is especially helpful in the early stages of 5v5 and 8v8 training, as it teaches players to stop "chasing the ball". To win, a team needs to cover the field efficiently, create new spaces of opportunity, and use the ball to turn those spaces into scoring chances. It's a drill that emphasizes passing and thinking over dribbling and running, helping players understand the larger possibilities that open up as the field and teams grow in size (see Figure 4.3).

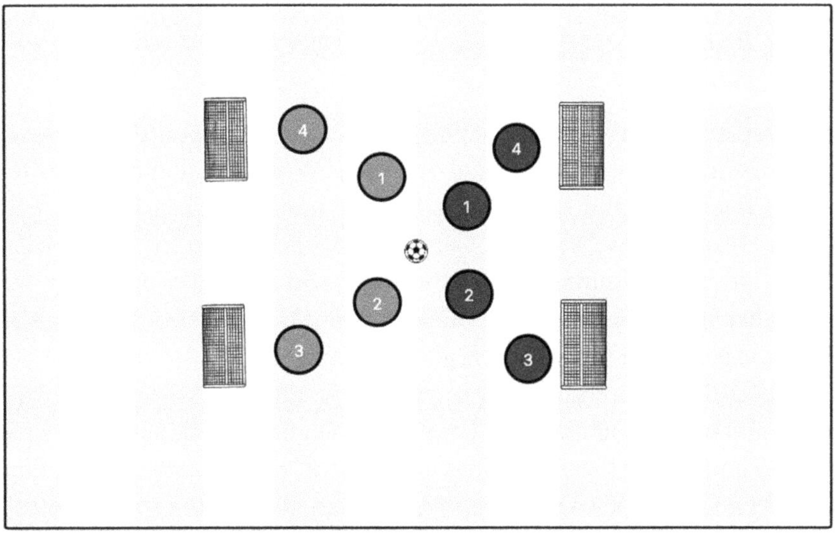

FIGURE 4.3 The Horst Wein minigame.

Even at the highest levels of professional football, decision-making—defined as players' ability to understand the various options in front of them and make suitable choices based on the situation—is something that requires training. In the mid-2010s, the German team Borussia Dortmund gained recognition for their use of the Footbonaut, a robotic cage that challenges players by launching balls at them, forcing them to control and return the balls to a randomly illuminated target square.[11] The Footbonaut is not a substitute for training; rather, it is a tool that helps players improve how their ball control skills can transfer into decision-making within a limited space of opportunity, since only one square lights up at a time. To develop as a football player is to learn to recognize more potential spaces and act within them through embodied skill. Technique and skills are tools that enable players to engage with the possibilities they perceive. When Johan Cruyff famously said that football is a "game that you play with your head, and legs are there to help", he was essentially explaining how the highest skill in the game is to perceive potential spaces and act on them most effectively. Great players are not those who can perform more tricks, but those who better understand the emerging spaces of opportunity ahead and make the right choices to navigate them. Similarly, great coaches are those who structure their teams' behavior so that through collective effort, a team creates advantageous spaces of opportunity while also neutralizing the opponent's attacking efforts. Coaching and playing football are all about understanding potential spaces. It is time to view the roles of coaches and players from a game design perspective.

FOOTBALL GREATNESS, EXPLAINED

Game design develops systems of rules that create possibility spaces for players to explore, allowing them to find the best solutions based on their skills to reach a goal they value. Game designers do not solely decide what players do at every moment—instead, they offer a set of tools within the possibility spaces shaped by the rules, and players customize these tools to enjoy the game in a way that feels good to them.

In football, the governing body responsible for the rules is the IFAB, a group that maintains and updates the Laws of the Game by making incremental changes and testing them at various tournaments before implementing final modifications. The IFAB can be seen as the "designers" of this sport. Football also undergoes play-testing, and some of its changes are softly launched, similar to mobile game development. Besides the IFAB, individual national associations can make certain rule adjustments within their development practices based on current pedagogical theories about the game.

If the IFAB and the local associations are the designers of the game, and the players are, well, the players, what is the role of coaches in football? Here's where game design theory can help us understand the beautiful game. A coach is a specific type of player who is dedicated to communicating to field players what the different possibility spaces are and how to act in them.[12] We have previously written about how player development can be understood using the concept of space of possibility. In that context, the role of a development coach is to communicate to players what the spaces of possibility are and how they can develop their skills so they can both perceive more spaces of possibility and make the right choices in them. However, the role of a team coach is different. Coaches need to develop an understanding of the different spaces of possibility they can explore with the team of players they are managing. Then they need to communicate and train their team to explore those spaces of possibility in matches.

Let's examine Pep Guardiola's coaching practices and philosophy as a case study. The following analysis is based on publicly available data about Guardiola's methods—as an ever-evolving coach, his approach has likely changed over time, and this may only represent one aspect of his career. That approach is centered on a single principle: ball possession. Guardiola's teams strive to retain possession, passing the ball quickly and accurately across the field, and recovering it swiftly after losing it to launch an attack against a disorganized opponent. His teams are heavily structured, play dynamically, and are systematic in how they occupy space.

Guardiola's understanding of the pitch divides it into 20 zones (see Figure 4.4). The goal of training is to teach the team to occupy these spaces so they can dominate the opposition in key zones, which are more likely to lead to goals. Between 2019 and 2023, there was a specific "Manchester City goal" that started with the team quickly switching the ball from side to side, followed by a quick one-two pass sequence between a player on the outer side of the pitch and another in the half-space between the outer side and the goal area. This allowed the winger to run into the box and make a cutback pass for a striker to tap in and score.

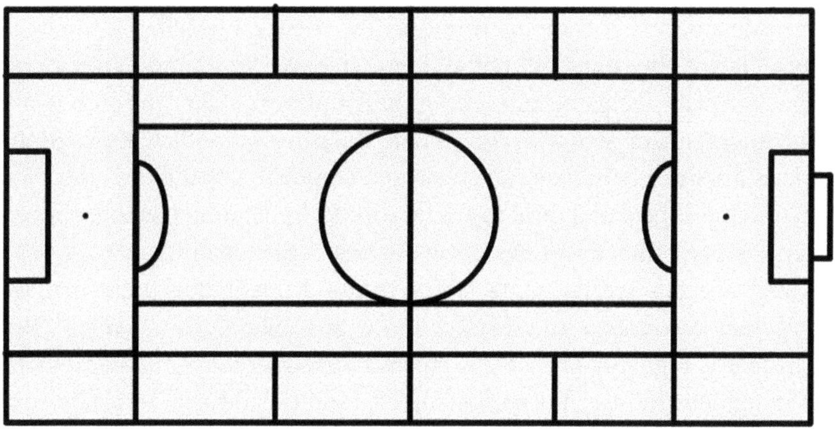

FIGURE 4.4 A diagram of the football pitch as used by Pep Guardiola in his drills in the 2010s and 2020s.

This "Manchester City goal" results from creating a space of opportunity through a series of movement patterns in the areas *between* the defending players of the opposing team. Attacking soccer relies on developing spaces where players can receive the ball under favorable conditions to shoot at goal. In Guardiola's teams, this creation of spaces of opportunity comes from quick passing among players positioned in areas formed by coordinated movement and the simultaneous placement of all players across the pitch.

Guardiola is just one example of the work coaches do to create spaces of possibility. When we consider the tactical tasks of coaching, we are actually observing a football coach's efforts to create spaces of possibility by utilizing individual and collective actions as tools. Football tactics result from coaches working with their team's skills and limitations within the rules of the game to occupy the pitch better, move the ball more efficiently, and achieve the goal of scoring while preventing the opposition from scoring. Coaches exploit spaces of possibility for their teams through tactical thinking and eliminate spaces of possibility for their rivals through defensive tactics.

This idea has a parallel in the world of video games. Players of competitive games such as Counter-Strike or DOTA often refer to the "meta" of the game. With this term, they mean tactical approaches that dominate a specific way of playing to achieve a goal. The concept of meta, which we will discuss in Chapter 7, has been well explained and studied by game designer Richard Garfield, the creator of the popular *Magic: The Gathering* card game.[13] In his view, metagaming involves anything outside the game rules that influences how the game is played. The idea has been adopted in esports to describe how some players develop tactics that can help them dominate the competitive scene. Meta occurs outside the gameplay experience. Engaging in the meta means playing the game, but not as a typical player. It is a more thoughtful interaction with the game rules, skills, and a player's ability to reach goals. Football coaches engage with the meta of the game of football; they see the game as a space where they can create and eliminate possibilities. Their job is to develop a meta and create a framework for generating possible options that players will then try to execute to the best of their abilities.

Great coaches see the meta, perceive novel possibilities, and manage teams that can create and exploit those possibilities in a game.[14] Pep Guardiola is arguably one of the greatest coaches of all time because he has redefined the way possession-based football and the occupation of spaces can lead to the creation of possibility spaces that ultimately lead to success. His master, Johan Cruyff, formulated the first modern iteration of positional play, himself developing the ideas of revolutionary coach Rinus Michels. While football fans have praised Jürgen Klopp for his high-intensity pressing game nowadays, his ideas can be traced back to Dinamo Kyiv coach Valeri Lobanovsky. And while José Mourinho and Diego Simeone perfected defensive tactics in the modern game, they are heirs to Helenio Herrera's realization that through the defensive destruction of the opponent's spaces of possibility, new attacking spaces open up, ready for a quick and disciplined team to occupy.[15]

Greatness in football coaching is then connected to the *creation* of spaces of possibility through the meta of the game, the astute understanding of how to utilize a team's skills more effectively to occupy spaces, thereby strengthening both individual and collective action to achieve the goal. Great coaches create spaces of possibility through tactical intervention in the game.

However, greatness in football, like in any sport, extends beyond coaches and their tactical interventions. What we love about the game, and any game, is the creativity and imagination of a player. Not their capacity to follow orders, but their capacity to create something new. From Marta to Messi, the greatest are always players who see what the rest of us have not seen, and act upon that. While a coach has the benefit of time and distance to formulate a meta that creates spaces of possibility, allowing players to express themselves and win the game, the greatest players of all time are those who, on the pitch, in real time, while playing, create new spaces of possibility.

Good players, even excellent players, can express themselves, but often only in the spaces of possibility that are afforded by the tactical work of a coach. Players have been trained to see and act upon *existing* spaces of possibility. But the truly great, the ones we watch the game for, create those spaces in real time. They defy tactical work, challenging the limits of skills and collective action, and suddenly act upon what they can only see. With their movement, ball skills, spatial reasoning, and pitch vision, they can be both coach and player during the game, creating new possibility spaces for themselves and their team. Greatness in football players depends on creating spaces of possibility.

By applying concepts from game design, we now have a framework to understand the different layers of play that occur in football. The game's designers, the IFBA, who are the custodians of the rules, revise and test these rules annually, implementing variations as the game evolves and faces challenges from technology or the athletes themselves. These rules provide the structure within which spaces of possibility can emerge. Coaches represent a specific type of player, dedicated to the meta of football. Their role involves understanding the rules, the players on the pitch, and how to optimize skills and space to create new possibility spaces that lead to success. The coach employs tactics to shape these spaces of possibility based on the game's rules. Players on the field execute those tactics, creating the beautiful, evolving patterns of movement and occupation of space over time that make football such a captivating game. Some players do not just execute actions within the possibility spaces created by coaches; they also create these spaces themselves. They are the greatest, the geniuses, the reason we keep returning to this sport, anticipating the unexpected and searching for fleeting moments of beauty when human skills in space bring something new to life, revealing a glimpse of what is possible that we didn't know existed.

THE DATA REVOLUTION AND ITS POSSIBILITY SPACES

Johan Cruyff once said:

> *I find it terrible when talents are rejected based on computer stats. Based on the criteria at Ajax now I would have been rejected. When I was 15, I couldn't kick a ball 15 meters with my left, and maybe 20 with my right. My qualities, technique and vision, are not detectable by a computer.*[16]

Cruyff is partially correct: a risk of the data revolution is that modalities of greatness that do not fit into computable data models are often ignored. In football, relying exclusively on data to make squad or tactical choices is making ill-informed decisions. Data is merely a means of understanding the game, and while it has helped move the game toward the future, many things remain invisible to data.

Concepts like possibility space and the knowledge accumulated in game design studies over the last few decades can help develop new data models and perspectives. While we won't be able to quantify greatness, possibility space does give us an indicator for what to look for in data. Many data indicators that are now currency in football, from expected goals to key passes, are all ways of finding the boundaries of possibility spaces as they are created and exploited in the game.

Let's examine the most popular football metric, expected goals. Besides indicating the quality of a shot a player takes, this metric also measures the movements and positions of players that reach or help create those scoring chances. Teams with high expected goals stats often build multiple potential scoring areas in the attacking zone, which their attackers then skillfully exploit.

We can see this metric, along with many others, as data points that identify specific events within the flow of the game. However, all these metrics function as tools to map the possible spaces of the game as it unfolds. They provide a way to see the boundaries of these spaces as they evolve, emphasizing the role of teams, tactics, and individuals in shaping the game. The data revolution in football is more than just new scouting tools—it offers a new way to view the game, helping us understand football in the context of other sports like baseball and basketball, as well as board games and video games. The data revolution lets us see the built-in structure of football, and how players and coaches, by working within the rules and expressing themselves through them, create the patterns that make the beautiful game.

NOTES

1 Salen and Zimmerman, 2003; Zubek, 2020.
2 Other games of this type are basketball, hockey, but also ultimate frisbee, and all variations of capture the flag. Invasion games are often used in classrooms to help develop an understanding of team-based logics and cooperation.
3 Wilson, 2008.
4 Sicart, 2008.
5 Clark and Anthropy, 2014.
6 For a reader who may want to enjoy other games besides football, we can only recommend both *Magic Maze* (https://boardgamegeek.com/boardgame/209778/magic-maze) and *Pandemic* (https://boardgamegeek.com/boardgame/30549/pandemic).
7 We explore this idea in depth in the chapter dedicated to the concept of emergence.
8 Chess' possibility space was measured by Claude Shannon as having 10^{120} possible games (using a game tree approach). With the same approach, Go has 10^{360} possible games.
9 Tobelius, 2019.
10 Boluk and Le Mieux, 2017.
11 Beavan et al., 2019.
12 Incidentally, most top-level coaches have been field players at a high level, like Guardiola and Arteta.
13 Elias et al., 2012.
14 Great players and even spectators, especially those who read endnotes in books about football, can also see the meta—a part of what makes them great at what they do.
15 This quick history of football tactics draws heavily from Jonathan Wilson's *Inverting the Pyramid* (Wilson, 2008) and from Michael Cox's *Zonal Marking* (Cox, 2019).
16 We have tried and failed to find the original source for this quote, so there may be a risk of it being apocryphal. In his book on Cruyff, Auke Kok mentions in passing Cruyff's skepticism of computers in refereeing (Kok, 2022, p. 471), but that's about the only reference we have for this issue. The quote however reflects Cruyff's understanding of the game and of coaching, and as such we consider it to be a valid opening for this coda.

CHAPTER 5

The Midfield

THINK OF A CIRCLE. In geometry, a circle comprises all points in a plane halfway from a central point known as the center. Now, shift your focus to a rectangle, which, in Euclidean geometry, is a quadrilateral characterized by four right angles. Lastly, envision a triangle, a polygon boasting three edges and three apexes (see Figure 5.1).

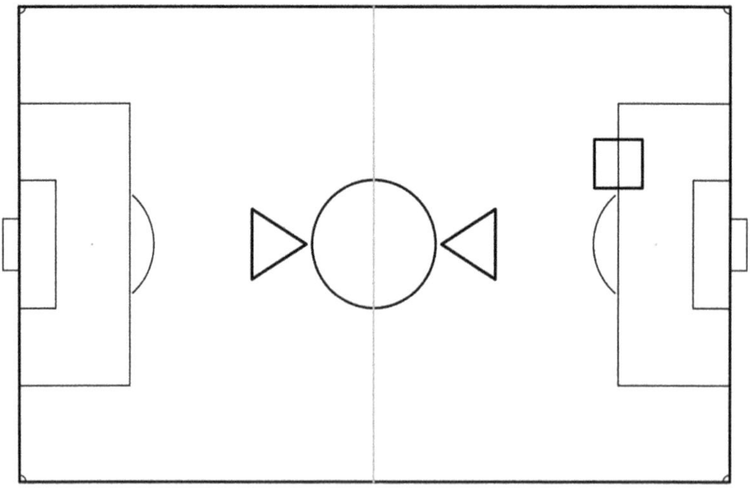

FIGURE 5.1 Three shapes and a football pitch.

DOI: 10.1201/9781003636762-6

However, let's put aside mathematics for a moment and explore these fundamental shapes. A circle may prompt thoughts of "the magic circle", a term coined by Dutch cultural theorist Johan Huizinga in his 1938 work *Homo Ludens* to explain the bounded time–space of play where ordinary life is suspended and special rules/meanings apply. The rectangle is the football pitch, the beloved arena of the game we enjoy watching. The triangle encourages us to delve into football tactics, pondering the exquisite strategies that shape the beautiful game.[1]

This chapter posits that football unfolds within Huizinga's magic circle. However, the modern football we know and embrace today wouldn't be complete without the evolution of the midfield. So, how did the midfield come to be? How does football unfold in and around this crucial area of the pitch? It does so through the art of running, strategic positioning, and precise passing, executed in triangular and rectangular movements and patterns. We will dive into the world of circles, squares, and triangles. We tell you how football's tactical evolution, centered on the midfield, relies on these basic shapes and movements within the magic circle of play. Yet, football is a dynamic and ever-evolving sport, prompting us to consider not just one "magic circle" but rather "magic *circles*".

THE MAGIC CIRCLE

Huizinga is the forefather of contemporary studies on games and play. As a scholar, he had an aesthetic approach to history, where art and spectacle played an important part. In his book *Homo Ludens*, with which he studies the phenomenon of play in culture, he proposed that all play takes place in a separate and special time and space. They are "forbidden spots" that are both located within the ordinary world and "dedicated to the performance of an act apart".

The backbone of culture, Huizinga declares, is play, and it is playing that drives culture forward. "Social life is endowed with supra-biological forms, in the shape of play, which enhances its value". He speaks of "the arena" in a double sense. On the one hand it refers to those "forbidden" and almost sacred places that separate the inside of the magic of play from the outside everyday life. On the other hand, the arena is connected to "the playground of the mind, in a world of its own which the mind creates for it".

You can play games on arenas made of stones or plastic, and you can play games inside your own head. And then, almost in passing, Huizinga mentions the concept of magic circle:

> *The arena, the card-table, the magic circle, the temple, the stage, the screen, the tennis court, the court of justice, etc., are all in form*

> *and function play-grounds [...] All are temporary worlds within the ordinary world, dedicated to the performance of an act apart*"[2]

Huizinga further states that for play to be considered authentic and meaningful to players and spectators, it must be fun, free of any obligations to society, and creative. He does not believe in a sharp line dividing work and goofing around. Play is independent of ordinary life; yet the scenery of play is acted out within real life. This is certainly the case of football stadiums. They are special, magical places—we call them "cathedrals" — despite being placed amid everyday life surroundings. It's also true of the football we play in the back garden, on the patio, or on the suburban street. At least, we can *make* them special through our imagination.

Space, time, and rules have one thing in common: they create order. Rules are absolute. To break them is to destroy the order and the play. Time signifies that play runs its course; it has a beginning and an end: in football, after 90 minutes plus additional time, or at the end of the tournament or the league season. And the space of games and sports feels almost like religiously ordered places.

However, a peculiar aspect of Huizinga's notion of play is that while he acknowledges that play is utterly absorbing and a dynamo of culture, he says in the same vein that play should only be taken seriously within the contest itself and not thereafter. This is relatively obscure and works against what every fan knows about football and from living with football. First, the game does not end once the referee blows the final whistle. It continues, dressed in arguments back and forth as to whether the striker was offside or onside, if the tactics were played out according to plan, if a lousy player should have been benched, and so on. When the game is interpreted, it knows no boundaries. Second, does the game suddenly stop or pause once people who have just watched it carries it outside the stadium or away from the screen? The zealous rant outside the magic circle is just as "serious" and "authentic" as inside it. Third, isn't it wrong to speak about the magic circle, in the singular sense? Especially since the game of football has utterly changed within the last 60 years.

MAN OF MIDFIELD: MÁRIO ZAGALLO

Herbert Chapman (1878–1934), famous for managing the English side Arsenal from 1925 to 1934, picked his own team and implemented his own tactics. He was a manager who believed in physical fitness and was one of the very first to introduce diet and fitness regimes, bringing in masseurs and physiotherapists to increase the well-being and stamina of his players.[3] Football in Europe was shambolic in the first half of the 20th century. There was no real midfield.

Coaches would often play in matches alongside the players they were supposed to manage. Communication about strategy between players were nonexistent. They would smoke, drink, consume unhealthy food, joke, or grumble about daytime jobs, take out their teeth before kick-off, and walk half across town to lousy changing rooms which the clubs couldn't afford themselves. Although things changed, tactically, with the arrival of the modern offside rule in 1925 (as we discussed in Chapters 1 and 2), football was still a rough sport with no real infrastructure or strategic manual and only recently separated from rugby. Chapman frequently commented to the press that no team he encountered attempted to organize a victory, let alone have a plan for the positioning of the players. So, he began to foster a tactical framework.[4]

He divided the field into "zones" and would insist that these zones would change once the actual game itself changed. To most ears, this was nonsense. Some British newspapers mockingly nicknamed him "the Philosopher". In the 1920s and 1930s football was played with two defenders, three midfielders, and five forwards (the "pyramid" or "WM" formation). Chapman began to drop midfielders down the field to bolster the defense. He added "inside" wingers and players operating in the spaces between midfield and attack, and all in all he tried to do more than just hoofing the ball up the pitch in the hope of finding a free attacker in the opponent's goal area (see Figure 5.2).

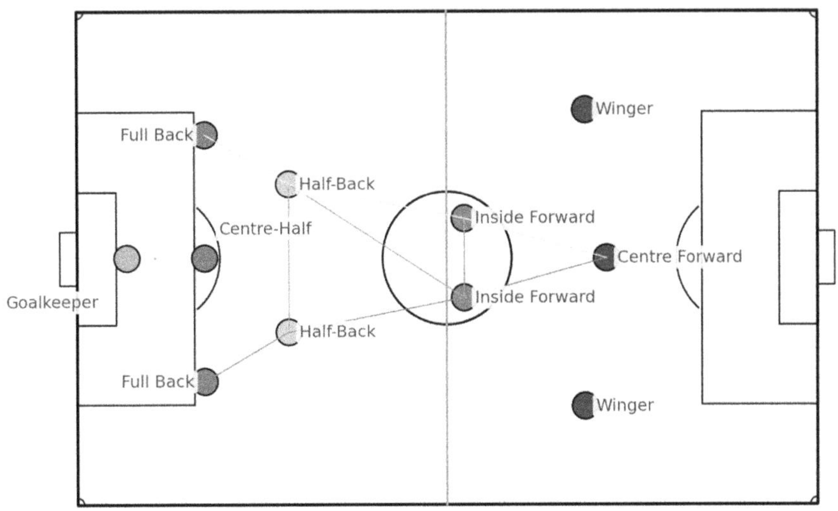

FIGURE 5.2 The WM formation.

In hindsight, Chapman was a steppingstone to football modernity. When did football become modern? In 1958, in Sweden, and it was the

Brazilian national team that invented the modern game.[5] The Brazilian team, led by Vicente Ítalo Feola, a sturdy man with slick hair, was put in a group with the former Soviet Union, England, and Austria. Arriving at the World Cup in Sweden in 1958, Feola introduced a 17-year-old Edson Arantes do Nascimento, better known as Pelé, to the world. This was the first and to date only time a non-European side had won a World Cup on European soil. The team trained in the town Hindås in Sweden during the tournament. The players, shaped in a 4-2-4 formation,[6] shun like diamonds: Santos, Orlando, Bellini, and ("the other") Santos as back four; Zito and Didi were the middle two; and Zagallo (left), Garrincha (right), Pelé, Vava (central) acted as attacking quartet. Pelé and Garrincha were not only instrumental in Brazil's success; they demolished Sweden in the final, which they won 5-2. They were also true media stars of their day.

And then there was Mário Zagallo, the "Old Wolf". He came from the Brazilian clubs Flamenco and Botafogo. Aymoré Moreira coached Brazil when they entered the World Cup in 1962, in Chile. Brazil beat Czechoslovakia 3-1 at the Estadio Nacional de Chile in the final. Moreira's dazzling move was to release Zagallo from the attack line and bring him down in a position slightly left of Zito and Didi. Moreira changed Feola's 4-2-4 to a 4-3-3 (so three in midfield rather than two). Zagallo still had the freedom to run forward (which he just couldn't resist), and he was also the link-up player between defense and offense. He made up for his lack of muscle mass with speed, fast movements, and remarkable tactical intelligence.

What kind of player was Zagallo? In 1962 there wasn't really a label for him. Today he would probably have been called a number 8, or a number 10, somewhere between Luka Modric and Neymar. Perhaps even a "false 10" as he would alternate between flank and middle, like today's stars Christian Eriksen or Kevin De Bruyne. Zagallo went on to win the World Cup in 1970 as manager of Brazil's national team.

Zagallo is so vital in modern football because he is that *extra* element that not only buttresses the midfield but adds organization and variation to it. Already in 1962, he was famed for his ability to execute attacks from deeper areas of the field. He reshaped the old game.

TRIANGLES AND SQUARES

By moving Zagallo just a few yards down the pitch, one could say, perhaps a bit lofty, that Moreira invented the midfield. The World Cup 1958 was a gamechanger, but it was foremost a game of conquer, as Brazil relied heavily on their top-four hard hitters (and a slice of luck). The year 1962 was conquer *and* command. Zagallo commanded the midfield—and as a result the game itself.

Zagallo and his new position also made way for the different roles assigned to midfielders. As the English say, there's the *destroyer* who defends, tackles, and steals the ball to jumpstart counterattacks. There's the *passer* who keeps the ball running and masters the fluent play. And, finally, there's the *creator*, the Zagallo character, the playmaker, or, as the Italians say, the *regista*.

The midfield makes the possibility space of the game explode.[7] Zagallo and his style of football also added an element of contingency. If they're skilled enough, players can always do more than what is robotically ascribed to their fixed position on the pitch. Here's an example: the number 9. That player is by convention the striker, the target forward, so he or she is programmed to score goals. And that's pretty much it, the trivial outcome of a functional job (what to do) and a spatial position (where to be). What becomes interesting in the era after Zagallo is a type of football, defined by the midfield, that surpasses the mere causality of the game.

There are roughly two shapes in football (after 1962): triangles and squares. They are archetypical, so of course there are bends and twists and innovations also. Belonging to the triangle mode is the Brazilian-Dutch game. It is perhaps best illustrated by Johan Cruyff, and because Cruyff exported his way of playing to Spain, it can also be found in the modern versions of Josep "Pep" Guardiola and Xavi Hernández.

It goes like this (think of a triangle while you read this): (1) pass the ball, (2) run into position, (3) get the ball. Or, if viewed from the receiver of that initial pass: (1) get the ball, (2) wait until a player has run into position, then (3) pass the ball (see Figure 5.3).

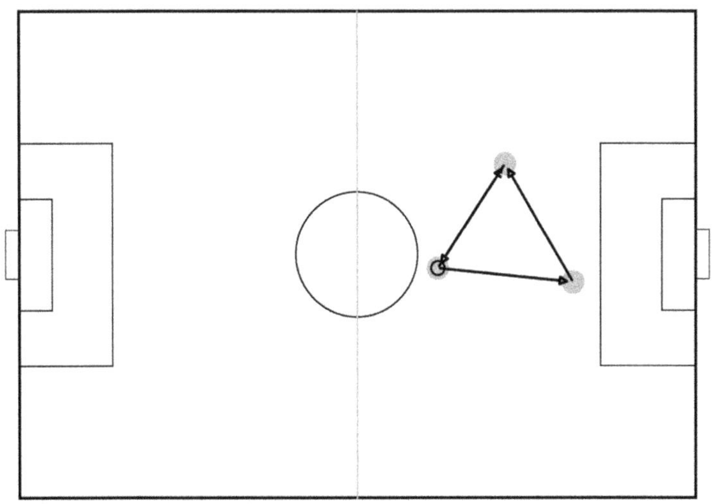

FIGURE 5.3 A triangular passing scheme.

Even the acclaimed one-two passing is really, when studied closely, a triangular movement: a player passes the ball, the other player runs into position and *then* receives the ball. The play in triangles is the result of the possibility space fostered by the new midfield (after 1962). To put it bluntly: without the new Zagallo midfield bravura, any triangularization would be pointless and stupid. Pass the ball, done! Give it to the number 9, and she'll score!

There's also the square. This one can see in English teams. It goes like this: (1) pass the ball, (2) pass the ball again, preferably to one of the flanks close to the sideline, (3) run up the flank, (4) make a pass into the opponent's goal area (see Figure 5.4).

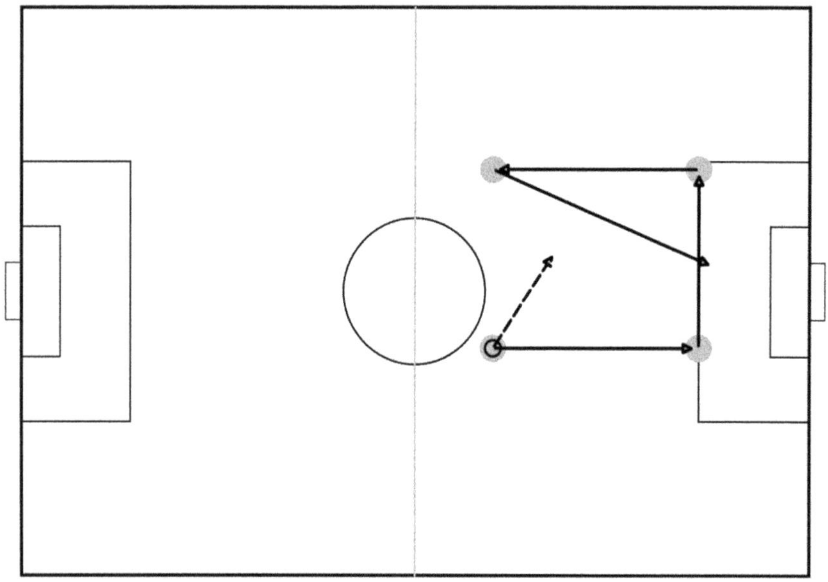

FIGURE 5.4 A square passing scheme.

When Leo Messi famously scored against Getafe in 2007 it was a carbon copy of Diego Maradona's second against England in the 1986 World Cup quarter final. It was a long, triangular run. The only thing Messi missed from the original was passing the ball to *himself* whilst sprinting into position and outsmarting all his opponents.

When Real Madrid's number 5, Zinedine Zidane, hammered his volley in the top corner of the goal in the Champions League final against Bayer Leverkusen, May 2002, it was effectively a squared ending. Zidane got the ball from Roberto Carlos on the flank following a series of very straight passes before that. Zidane took the ball "from out of the air", as one British commentator lamented, and scored.

Johan Cruyff was a life-long advocate of playing in triangles, and we turn to him now also to discuss how the midfield shifts the focus from goal scoring to mastery of space. And what about football in itself? Is it a functional design or an artform? Let's find out.

A DESIGNER'S GAME

The football pitch is a space some 100 meters long and 50 meters wide. In the two opposite ends stands a goal which is about seven meters wide and 2.5 meters high. As Justin Reynolds remarks in his essay "Johan Cruyff and the poetics of space", this is a rather claustrophobic place where there isn't much room to roam about and kick a ball.[8] Chapman added inside wingers. Feola relied on four guys to score goals, and Moreira inserted Zagallo in his gameplan, thus inventing the modern midfield.

Cruyff brought a designer's eye to the game. For Cruyff, as for any designer, "the challenge was to make intelligent use of limited space, in this case, a football pitch", Reynolds writes. As a player for Ajax and the Dutch national team, and later as manager of FC Barcelona, Cruyff was a tower of speed and thought as opposed to strength and physicality.[9] In the 1970s his playing was conveyed and marketed as hippie-cool while in fact it was orderly and highly rational. It consisted in quicksilver triangular patterns that would probe the opposition's defenses. Back then it was called "total football", and it was laid out as players' ability to replace any other player on the pitch (except the goalkeeper).

A player should always be able to do more than what is just required by function or position. Cruyff demanded that a player should think passing and running as one movement across the pitch, commanding his pace and vision of the game most resourcefully and economically. Players must be able to control the space around them—"move the air", as Cruyff said—and dictate the game's time. Even today, students of La Masia, Barcelona's academy, are told from day one that it's all about moving to the right spot at the right *time*. When Cruyff was slow, the game was slow. When he ran, the game was frantic. Cruyff was the clockwork of the game.

Maybe it simply has to do with the Dutch geography. David Winner writes in his book *Brilliant Orange*:

> *Space is an inordinately precious commodity, and for centuries the use of every square centimetre of every Dutch city, field and polder*

> *has been carefully considered and argued over. The land is controlled because as a matter of national survival it must be. The Dutch water system has to be regulated tightly because more than fifty per cent of the country is below sea level. In the west of the country the entire landscape is man-made.*[10]

THE MIDFIELD AS A CUNNING ARTFORM

The Argentinians admire the Dutch, especially Cruyff. They call the Dutch football "clockwork orange", a title that plays on Anthony Burgess' novel *Clockwork Orange* from 1962. The Netherlands trashed Argentina 4-0 at the World Cup in 1974. But the South Americans play and narrate the game differently.

In his book *Inverting the Pyramid*, Jonathan Wilson tells the story of how the original English game developed quite differently in Central Europe, particularly Hungary, and South America's Argentina and Chile.[11] In Hungary football became a "waltz" (the triangle again), a feminized athleticism as opposed to the South Americans who favored *machismo* and the entertaining gambit. Wilson quotes an anecdote from the novel by Ernesto Sábato, *Sobre Héroes y Tumbas*, in which a player eagerly awaits applause after scoring a goal. His manager is unsatisfied with the goal and responds, "Yes, but I did not have fun".

Sábato's scene shows why Argentina loves cunning skillfulness. Forget about the Hungarian's aesthetics and the efficient triangles of the Dutch. In Argentina, there's an element of tango in football. One such element is the *sacada*, performed by the leading man, derived from the verb "sacar" which literately means "take away" or "remove". Argentina's football is a game of displacement, of removing the opponent's obstacles, making fun of him and penetrating his walled defenses. It's almost like courting a woman whilst displaying masculine sexuality. It's a clockwork—tik-tok tik-tok—but also an art of deception.

There's a word for that in Italian football (Italy having many strong bonds with Argentina, trade, and shipping not least). The word is *furbizia*. It stands for doing tricks, pulling a stunt, mastering a con. The Argentinian playmaker, their number 10, evolved into the *enganché*, literally "the hook".[12] Diego Maradona was the most famous hook of them all. He placed himself in the space between midfield and offence, but he had the freedom to work as a second striker.

And here's the catch: the Dutch are designers who *make* plays, like an architect drawing a house by controlling the space around it. He's a play-*maker.*

The Argentinian playmaker, the hook, is an artist (or a con man), who very macho *plays* the game. He's a *play*-maker.

Both score goals, obviously. But as Ernesto Sábato asked: did it look good?

CLOCKWORK AND ART

Here's an example of Dutch clockwork followed by Argentinian cunningness. It's June 16, 2006. The World Cup has just begun, and Argentina meets Serbia and Montenegro on Veltins-Arena in Gelsenkirchen, Germany. The blue-and-whites have a fantastic team: Pablo Aimar, Juan Román Riquelme, Maxi Rodrigues, Javier Saviola, Hernán Crespo, Esteban Cambiasso—and an 18-year-old teenager by the name of Leo Messi.

They all play a part in the 2-0 goal. A total of 25 passes, before Crespo drops a back-heel pass, a *sacada*, that completely makes buffoons of the Serbes. It takes away their feet, just like in tango. The ball from Crespo lands at Cambiasso who blazes it into the back of the net.

David Brillinger has written an article on this very goal and the build-up to it in *Journal of Quantitative Analysis in Sports*. He claims that it's a bright example of the superiority of the midfield. It shows how the flow of modern football were expressed in Argentina's luscious goal.[13]

"It was almost like *futsal*", Crespo, the chap with the back-heel, claimed afterwards in an interview with the Italian newspaper *La Gazzetta dello Sport.*

The beauty of the Argentinian 2-0 goal is that despite all the efforts made by the opponent's team to disrupt their diligent play, take away the danger, in the end, no pass of Argentina's turned out to be a bad one. They all clicked together as a piece of sneaky clockwork artfully crafted to "take away" the Serbian foot. In football, a natural law is that every move and action run the danger of being a bad one.[14] Argentina not only commanded the possibility space by triangulating the ball from post to post, but they also proved the point of the midfield: that it is *the* place where football is coordinated, just like Zagallo had envisioned. Back and forth, tik-tok, tik-tok, clockwork orange. As the manager in *Sobre Héroes y Tumbas* would say: "Yes, and I had lots of fun".

Crespo performs one of the hardest and most entertaining stunts in football, the back-heel pass. It looks like art and could have gone wrong, but it didn't. It's contingency to the max, a masterful exploit of possibility space.

And that's why the Argentinians love the Dutch recipe: neat triangular passes, and to top it, that little spicy, cunning extra at the very end: a tango back-heel.

MAGIC CIRCLES

At the beginning of this chapter, we asked three questions concerning Johan Huizinga's claim that the "magic circle" only lasts as long as the contest itself.

1. Does the game extend beyond the game?
2. Can the game be carried outside the stadium or the screen and still be part of the game?
3. Does football have only one magic circle—or should we rather talk of magic circles?

The first question is about *time*. Along with space, time is the dimension that orders play, keeps play civilized, and provides it with culture. But in football (and probably within all sports), the game does not end once the actual, physical match finishes. On the contrary, it explodes in the fan culture that surrounds football, both positively and negatively, as we'll explore in Chapter 8. The match is but one element in a large network and franchise of entertainment, which we'll investigate in Chapter 9. It extends into interpretations, judgments, predictions, rumors, and biases around the globe—and even into the book you are reading right now. All of this is part of football's magic circle.

The second question is about *space*. There are arenas made of concrete matter, usually build outside towns, and once we're there, they feel like churches or cathedrals. This is the ritualistic and almost religious sensation of games, Huizinga ponders. However, we carry the church with us—just like in most religions that are supposed to be "mobile". The game can easily be transported outside the stadium or away from the screen.[15] It's that "stretchy" quality of sports games that fans fancy.

The third question is about *evolution*. The evolution of the midfield, from Mário Zagallo to Leo Messi, from Zito and Didi to Kevin De Bruyne, from a region of the pitch that is just run over to a region where every aspect of the game is orchestrated—all this test Huizinga's "magic circle" to the limit. Today, we would not see a circle (or we would not feel that we were part of one) if we watched a game of football from before 1962. Imagine a match between Leeds and Wolverhampton, a dim Saturday afternoon, loads of kick and rush, unsophisticated yelling, a turf full of holes, and a thick smell of fish and chips in the air. It would be an alien circle, at the very least, a clutter of bodies maladroitly hounding a ball without paying any attention to the midfield.

What follows from those answers is not a rejection of Huizinga so much as a pluralization. Football today is made of circles. Some are concentric, some overlap like a Venn diagram, some travel. There is the cathedral circle of the stadium; the broadcast circle of cameras, commentary, and replays; the regulatory circle of IFAB, referees, assistants, and the off-site VAR room that literally projects an external chamber back into the match; the economic circle of platforms, sponsors, and tours; the data circle of tracking, expected goals, and performance models; the supporter circle that lives in pubs, group chats, and marches; and, inside the rectangle, micro-circles of practice—the rondo, the huddle, the second-ball swarm. None of these closes neatly when the whistle goes. They get bigger and smaller across the week.

The midfield is where these circles touch. It is the hinge between the sealed ritual of the 90 minutes and the porous networks that surround them. Training builds a player's perceived possibility space on Tuesday. The analyst's report narrows likely patterns on Thursday. On Sunday a midfielder decides, in a third of a second, whether that pattern still holds. A rondo's tiny circle becomes a press-resistance pocket under the South Stand; a set of clips on a tablet becomes a cue to step into the half-space; and a law written by a committee becomes a body-shape rule of thumb: open to the field, receive on the back foot, move the air. The circle of play is therefore not a wall but a membrane.

This plural view also explains why the exact match can be lived as different circles at once. In the away end the circle is pilgrimage and noise. Meanwhile, on the bench it is chess with substitutions. In the VAR booth it is a forensic lab. On the timeline it is a meme factory. And for the *regista*, the Italian number 10, it is a book to be read at pace. When Zagallo dropped 10 meters in 1962, he did not just redraw a formation. No, he relocated the center of translation between circles. He made midfield the game's interpreter.

If we keep Huizinga's insight, that play creates a fenced in almost sacred world apart, but treat the "apart" as layered rather than singular, football's history stops contradicting him and starts extending him. The modern game is not one circle but *a field of circles with the midfield as its relay station*. That is why contemporary spectators feel the game everywhere: in their bodies in the ground, in their phones on the tram, in their arguments at work, and in their children's 3v3 drills. The magic is not diluted by multiplicity. It is produced by it.

NOTES

1 Though one might argue in favor of the square, like Portuguese coach Ruben Amorim, or FC Barcelona legend Xavi Hernández. We will not take sides here, but we'll return to the square later in the chapter.

2 Johan Huizinga: *Homo Ludens: A Study of the Play Element in Culture*. Beacon, 1955 (orig. 1938), p. 10.

3 Jamie Ward: "The Forgotten Pioneers of Football: Herbert Chapman", *Bleacherreport.com*, Jan. 2, 2009.

4 Patrick Barclay: *The Life and Times of Herbert Chapman: The Story of One of Football's Most Influential Figures*. W&N, 2015.

5 There were tactical heaves leading to Brazil's triumph in 1958: England saw the rise of a 4-3-3 system, pioneered by manager Alf Ramsey. The system consisted of a corpus of hard-working men chasing the ball uncompromisingly completely devoid of any aristocratic individualism. Ramsey did not believe in stars; he trusted workers. Karl Rappan, Austrian coaching genius, introduced the sweeper in the 1950s, a central defender that could run up the pitch and take part in attacks or fall back as a last post. Hungary, everybody's darling team in the postwar era, even toyed with a false number 9. In the Italian *metodo*, derived from Vittorio Pozzo's 3-5-2, the sweeper morphed into the libero.

6 Since 1958 the 4-2-4 formation has not returned to the tactical boards (as it quickly developed into the British 4-4-2 with flanks, and the Italian 4-4-2 diamond). *Until*, and this is a remarkable history loop, the FIFA World Cup 2006 in which Ronaldinho, Kaka, Ronaldo Nazario, and Adriano shined as a magic foursome. Brazil's 2006 line-up was effectively a classic 4-2-4.

7 Game scholar Will Wright defines the possibility space as "a site of constant but productive, generative conflict between order and chaos, between rules and uninhibited play" (Will Wright: "Sculpting Possibility Space" (2004), http://itc.conversationsnetwork.org/shows/detail376.html).

8 Justin Reynolds: "Cruyff and the Poetics of Space" (March 2016), justinreynoldsessays.com.

9 Liam Shannon: *Point of Attack: Johann Cruyff, Sun Tzu & The Art of War in Football*. Independently published, 2021.

10 David Winner: *Brilliant Orange. The Neurotic Genius of Dutch Football*. Bloomsbury Publishing, 2000.

11 Jonathan Wilson: *Inverting the Pyramid – A History of Football Tactics*. Orion Books, 2008.
12 Eduardo Archetti: *Masculinidades: Fútbol, polo y tango en la Argentina*. CreateSpace Publishing, 2016.
13 David Brillinger: "A Potential Function Approach to the Flow of Play in Soccer". *Journal of Quantitative Analysis in Sports*, 3/1, 2007, 1–19.
14 See Hans Ulrich Gumbrecht: "Epiphany of Form: On the Beauty of Team Sports". *New Literary History*, 30/2, 1999, pp. 351–372, for a scrutiny of this vital aspect of sports.
15 Social realism and a quasi-religious life with football comes together in Maria Giese's 1996 film *When Saturday Comes*. It portrays Jimmy Muir, played by Sean Bean, who completely orients his hard-drinking brewery worker life in Sheffield, England, by football without having the discipline and the audacity to make anything of it. Muir craves for Saturday's matches, a desire brought down from father to son. Those matches seem the only stable happenings that make sense in a world with far too many choices and failures. See also Geoff Pearson: *An Ethnography of English Football Fans: Cans, Cops and Carnivals*. Manchester University Press, 2012.

CHAPTER 6

Football Is a Game of Emergence: Or Is It?

In chapter 1 we defined the possibility space as the realm of actions the laws of football make available at any instant, and the ways players and coaches continually explore that realm. Players, teams, and coaches strive to accomplish their goals at a given moment. For example, when a winger receives the ball wide in a 4-3-3, the fullback might overlap, and the striker will run toward the goal area. Add to that the support of the number 8 further down the pitch. Together they create a small triangle of options: carry inside, play the overlap, slide past the defender. As teams rehearse this pattern, they learn which branch most often yields a shot. It could be the cut-back to the arriving number 8, say, Jude Bellingham of Real Madrid, and then the open possibility set begins to harden into a few likely choices. A possibility space is never static, unless it is viewed from above, frozen in time. It evolves during gameplay as players' skills develop, enabling them to perceive, comprehend, and pursue new objectives.

Over time players will learn how to master the possibility space and discover efficient pathways to navigate it. Thereby, the possibility space transforms into a *probability space*. The science behind measuring probability is that an event *can* happen. The probability (P) of an event (A) is therefore a quantification of how likely it is that the event will happen: P(A).

DOI: 10.1201/9781003636762-7

Gamers use probability to determine the chances of certain outcomes—landing on a specific square in a board game or drawing a particular card from a deck. The trick about understanding probability is to know how to make informed decisions about which actions to take to improve the chances of winning.

In this sense, football can be viewed as a dynamic feedback system. Each action taken, each pass, feint, run, or interception feeds back into the larger system of play, modifying future possibilities. Cybernetics is the study of control and communication in animals, machines, and organizations through feedback loops.[1] Football is an example of cybernetics in motion; a physical system that regulates itself via feedback loops and a continual readjustment of behavior based on immediate outcomes. A player overhits a pass? The loop closes. They recalibrate next time. Tactical systems evolve in real time and are influenced by this incessant flow of corrections.

This chapter will delve into the intricacies of football's probability space, shedding light on its significance. We will demonstrate how the game studies concept *emergence* is intimately intertwined with it. Emergent properties are defined as the unexpected results of the relationship between the parts of a system and their environment. In football, sometimes those emergent properties lead to bad luck, and sometimes they can be beneficial. We shall provide arguments and examples for two very basic ideas that thrive in the game of football:

1. Once you master the game (by playing it or watching it), the possibility space narrows more and more down to a probability space.
2. Once you master the game (by playing or watching it), what begins with feels like an emergent, nonlinear space, becomes more and more a linear progression space.

To elucidate these ideas, we will introduce a unique game of our own invention that you will exclusively encounter within the pages of this book: The Game of Switches.

THE GAME OF SWITCHES

Football is a high-pressure game of how options turn into decisions. In the Game of Switches, you should think of each room as a game state. The switches are the actionable options available at that moment. The timer and the traps stand for urgency and risk. And, finally, the opened door is a locally successful outcome that immediately creates a new state with new options. The "right" switch in one room may be wrong in the next, not because the player forgets, but because the system updates. It's a hard game with many options and high stakes. Just like football.

Miguel wakes up and finds himself trapped in a room filled with switches. A voice tells him that to escape, he must find the right switch. Miguel tries one switch after another, but to no avail. The door at one end of the room remains stubbornly shut. Finally, through a stroke of luck, he finds the correct switch, and with a rasping sound, the door opens. Miguel enters the next room, only to discover another set of switches. After hours of searching, he collapses. Room 17 is where he made it to.

Miguel is a whimsical adult-child who cannot resist the temptation to toggle every switch he encounters. However, he must resist this urge, especially since each room conceals deadly traps that activate after a fixed amount of time. Miguel realizes that this is a game of unraveling causality, of carefully examining rooms, switches, and the spaces between them to unlock the path through the maze.

If there's such a thing as the beginning of a game, it would be the switch. Game scholar Hans-Joachim Backe demonstrates "how narrative acts as a structuring device for ludic processes", so that a vital narrative object can serve as a call to action.[2] Our switch becomes a call to action ("press me!", it says), the play button. It plunges the player into a conflict that calls for strategic thinking and navigational skills, to think and to move. Miguel encounters an overwhelming realm of possibilities, with countless switches and potential incorrect actions. He sees an open-ended world, where anything could happen. He sees emergence. How advantageous it would be, he thinks to himself, to acquire the tactics to navigate successfully!

Being a skilled computer gamer, after some time, Miguel becomes adept at the game. He begins to perceive the world as linear and comprehends the necessary course of action.[3] There is a fair chance he will survive. He has uncovered his probability space.[4] This is a space that contains the actions he should probably take, in a certain order and manner, to achieve the desired outcome.

Once Miguel has gained entrance to the probability space, he is more likely than ever to find what economists studying game theory refer to as a dominant strategy that will also lead to a dominant path:[5] thinking the right way, moving the right way (and in hindsight, the *only* way). If Miguel wishes to escape (or rather, find the exit room with the exit switch), he must press certain switches, avoid others, and move in specific directions.

Miguel's journey is not just about learning a dominant strategy—it is about aligning perception with causality (see Figure 6.1). In this regard, his understanding is modeled not unlike how a scientist or engineer might engage with a complex system: through the formulation and iterative adjustment of a model.[6] This is where scientific reasoning and game mechanics, and most importantly: football, begin to converge. Just as a scientific model is never complete but useful in reducing uncertainty,[7] Miguel's mental model of the game allows him to navigate it efficiently. The goal is not omniscience (to see everything) but operability (to locate the right path). Similarly, in football, no player or coach sees the whole system at once. Instead, they operate through evolving tactical models, internal, partial representations refined through feedback and performance.

We will dig deeper into the concept of emergence shortly. For now, let's revisit the two fundamental ideas introduced at the beginning of this chapter:

1. Miguel's proficiency in playing the Game of Switches improves significantly, enabling him to refine the expansive possibility space into a more manageable probability space.
2. Miguel's understanding of how to navigate the game—navigating through rooms and switches—continues to grow, gradually transforming what appeared to be an open-ended space into a structured and progressive environment.

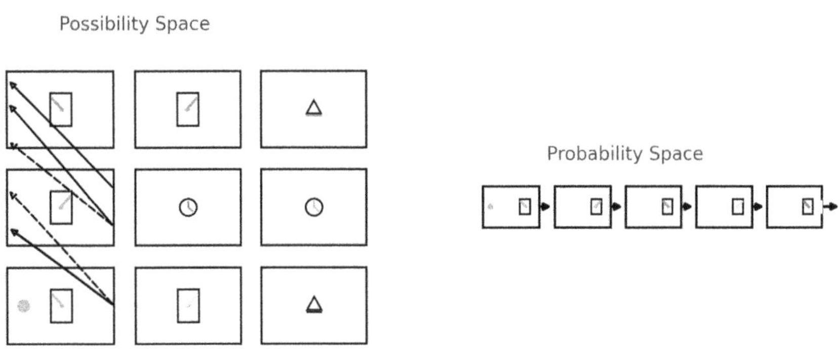

FIGURE 6.1 Left panel: a 3 × 3 maze of rooms with multiple switches, timers, traps, and branching: many options and risk/urgency. Right panel: a linear corridor of rooms with one clear forward path and an exit—showing how learned patterns narrow into progression.

GAME STATES

When you play a game (analogue or digital), various times exist. In computer science, they are referred to as states.[8] A system, such as a computer game, or the Game of Switches, is considered stateful when designed to retain information about preceding events or interactions. The collective set of states that a system can occupy is known as its state space. This is also referred to as the possibility space, as we discussed in Chapter 4.

States represent moments in time. Suppose we designate Miguel's initial encounter with the Game of Switches as "t1". At this point, he views the world before him as a chaotic realm of endless possibilities, teeming with countless exit routes. Now, let's advance to "t2". At this juncture, we encounter a transformed Miguel, one who has immersed himself in the game, uncovering its dominant strategy and dominant path through the recollection of past interactions. His mastery of the game comprises three essential skills:

1. He turns the possibility space into a probability space.
2. He turns emergence into progression.
3. He learns from t1 to t2.

From a cybernetic perspective, this is precisely what feedback loops accomplish: they allow a system to learn from itself. Miguel's switches are inputs; his observations of success or failure are outputs. Through feedback, his actions are recalibrated. The feedback loop, far from being just a mechanical metaphor, is a key to understanding how knowledge emerges in games.

EMERGENCE AND PROGRESSION

In his essay "The Open and the Closed: Games of Emergence and Games of Progression", Jesper Juul discusses the fundamental shapes of computer games.[9] He identifies two categories: games of emergence and games of progression. Games of emergence are characterized by simple rules that combine to create varied gameplay experiences. These include card and board games, as well as most action and strategy games. They have a limited number of rules, are often straightforward, and provide numerous variations and strategies for players to explore. On the other hand, games of progression require players to complete a predefined set of actions to reach the end goal. In these games, the game designer has more control over the sequence of events, often driven by cinematic or storytelling ambitions.

Football is a game of emergence, and so are videogames like *Counter-Strike* or *Far Cry*, because players need more than just a rulebook. They also need a strategic manual. Conversely, when playing a game of progression that guides players along a predetermined path, a "walkthrough" is the most efficient tool (although it often feels a bit like cheating). A walkthrough is a step-by-step guide that tells players exactly how to progress through a game, what to do, where to go, and how to solve puzzles or beat challenges. It often includes optimal routes, secrets or collectibles, and boss strategies, and it usually contains spoilers. Juul's distinction between emergence and progression allows us to analyze games that offer players a wealth of choices and paths (games of emergence), as well as games that subtly or not so subtly guide players toward specific goals and rewards (games of progression).

The cybernetic lens adds nuance to this distinction. While a game may appear emergent in structure, its progression emerges from iterative feedback loops within the player. What is progression if not a subjective stabilization of emergent complexity into reliable patterns? The player becomes a regulator of uncertainty, sifting signal from noise, pruning the irrational in favor of the probable. This mirrors how models in science are used not to simulate everything, but to allow coherent interaction with complex systems. Football is too intricate to be fully knowable, but strategic modeling (like in game AI or match analytics) makes it playable, as we saw in Chapter 3. Thus, football is what philosophers would call an epistemic system, where players, coaches, and fans co-construct meaning through performative trial, error, and interpretation. The system never closes, but the loop tightens.

But Juul's terminology, as we saw above, is formalistic. It focuses on the structure of games and their differences rather than how they are experienced. Here's the evolution of the game if all things go well:

A. A switch = a ludic action = "press me!"

B. Combination of switches (probability space).

C. Right outcome = most successful navigation = learning from t1 to t2.

A system that contains operability, knowledge, and perhaps most importantly memory is precisely able to deal with these three parameters: it sees objects (switches, a ball, other players); it increasingly knows how to handle these objects (hit a switch, pass the ball); and it is capable of refining its actions aimed at desired outcomes through memory that ideally makes everything better and cooler at t2 than at t1. Systems that are able to do all of this, especially rely on adaptive memory, are called *recursive systems*. The trick here is to think of the footballer (or Miguel, the Game of Switches player) as a system, thereby excluding rather important stuff like emotionality, passion for the game, fear of losing, and so on.

A footballer, feeling overwhelmed by the possibility space of the pitch, might exclaim, "I'm lost! Who should I pass the ball to?" If this was the Game of Switches, it would be, "Oh my God, there are so many switches! I can't figure this out!". All the while the clock ticks.

However, when the myriad possibilities are channeled into actions that are most likely to yield the desired outcome, the nature of the game changes—from a game characterized by emergence to one driven by progression. This shift unfolds gradually, through a process of trial and error, coupled with the refinement of gameplay, transitioning from t1 to t2. Effective moves are replicated, while undesirable ones are avoided. Football begins as a game of emergence and matures into a game of progression. (Recall Chapter 4's discussion of youth training as a means to narrowing and tightening the possibility space.)

A GAME OF EMERGENCE—OR WAS IT?

It's the first leg of the men's UEFA Champions League round of 16 tie, February 21, 2022. Liverpool, playing on their home turf, faces Real Madrid in a classic game. In a stunning display of skill, Darwin Núnez scores just four minutes into the match with a cool flick, following some sharp movements from Mohamed Salah. Ten minutes later, Salah takes advantage of Real Madrid goalkeeper Thibaut Courtois's ham-fisted footwork, making it 2-0. Then, out of nowhere, Real's Vinicius Junior cuts into the goal area and curls the ball into the net, bringing the score to 2-1. Fifteen minutes later, Liverpool keeper Alisson Becker's clearance unintentionally goes in off Vinicius, leveling the score at 2-2. In the second half, Madrid scores three more goals, setting the final score at 2-5.

How can we describe this in line with the pairing of concepts explained above? If we write it like a formula it would read something like: possibility -> probability; emergence -> progression; t1 -> t2.

The lazy answer, which football journalists do all the time, is to resort to club mythology. Ah, this is one of those "great European nights", the *remontadas*, the comebacks, the cyclical nature of history. Faced against the wall, Real Madrid always wins. And so on.

But this is how the game is narrated. These are examples of readymade storytelling, of how the game of football is habitually conveyed to an audience. Our job is to understand the undergirding mechanics of the match and how it progressed. Not merely myth, not only chaos. The match—like Miguel's rooms—is a system. And if it is a system, it means it can feed back into itself. Every goal, every error, becomes part of a self-regulating loop that shapes what comes next. In this sense, football is neither wholly emergent nor fully progressive. It is a cybernetic spiral, tightening through play, data, and experience. The first half of the Liverpool–Real Madrid match was a game of emergence. It felt chaotic, as if both teams got entangled in a vicious swamp of anything-can-happen.

Yet this is the result of you populating the game at t1 and asking yourself how it might have felt like. The answer: chaotic, full of emergence, way too much possibility space.

Let's instead rewind first half of the match from a cooler, strategic perspective. We lay out all the states, t1, t2, t3, and so forth, as moments and points within the game. What we find is a sequential order, a pattern. It goes like this:

Liverpool 1-0, dazzling. Liverpool 2-0, fortunate.
Real Madrid 2-1, dazzling. Real Madrid 2-2, fortunate.

We call "dazzling" A and "fortunate" B. Then we have the following scheme:

AB/AB

In football commentaries, phrases like "bad luck", "almost magical", or "destiny" are often heard. The team had an awful day; or the team just clicked together. And maybe this was really misfortune and magic, one for each team. However, what the Liverpool-Madrid example shows us, scientifically, is a structural change from chaos to order, from blurbs of emergence to a steady pattern.

Look closer at the 2-2 goal, where Becker tries to clear the ball, fails, and Vinicius scores (see Figure 6.2). The likelihood of an event happening is defined as the function of P to A, P(A), where P is probability and A is the event. For an event to be successful (result in a goal), we number it "1". So now we have P(1). The job in football, for the players and for the manager, is to increase P as much as possible to make it "equalize" A. 0,9(1) is way better than 0,2(1). Let's pretend that Vinicius didn't pick up on the signs and signals of the game. At this point, it was tense and error-ridden. Perhaps he would have placed himself further away from the Liverpool goal area. Mathematically: 0,2(1). No chance on Earth to score from there. But he was vigilant and adapted well to the game; he saw a dominant path through the possibility space; he anticipated a rich likelihood of success by moving from one state (t1) to another (t2); suddenly he was much closer to Becker (rather, he didn't' leave the goal area in the first place)—and voila: P(A) = 0,9(1). Goal!

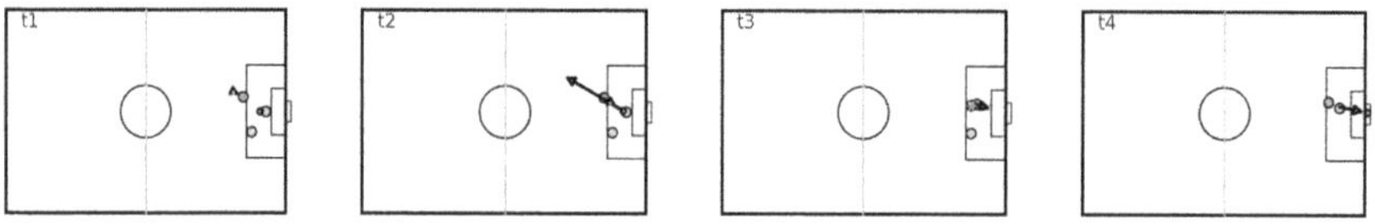

FIGURE 6.2 A sequence of the Real Madrid goal against Liverpool.

Consider another example: the famous 2014 World Cup semi-final between Germany and Brazil, in which Germany stunned the world with a 7-1 victory. On paper, the match started as an evenly matched contest between two footballing giants. But within the first 30 minutes, Germany had already scored five goals. If we were to assess the game mid-first-half, say at t2, we would be watching a complete collapse in real time—an emergent event unfolding too quickly for the Brazilian team, the commentators, or even the fans to process. The possibility space, which should have included Brazil's home advantage, their technical flair, and the backing of a passionate crowd, was suddenly overridden by a new progression. It was as though the probability function P(A) was recalibrating on the fly: with each German goal, the emergent pattern became a ruthless progression, the chaos tilting into inevitability.

And yet, when we watch the game retrospectively—when we construct the linear playback from t1 to t7 (seven goals)—it no longer looks like emergence. It becomes a sequence. Müller scores: t1. Klose scores: t2. Kroos scores: t3 and t4. Khedira scores: t5. Schürrle adds two more: t6 and t7. The game is narrated back to us as structured, even surgical. The very violence of the event becomes understandable in hindsight. Emergence is thus retroactively rewritten as progression.

This leads to a fundamental paradox of football: the simultaneous coexistence of two temporalities. On the one hand, there is the linear temporality of replay, narrative, and structured time where every t1 leads rationally to a t2. This is the domain of the commentator, the analyst, and the fan watching on Monday morning. This is the order of sequence, pattern, and causal logic. On the other hand, there is the immersive temporality of emergence. This is the view from within the field, from the player's perspective making a split-second decision, or the fan feeling the stadium pulse shift unpredictably. This temporality is unstructured, a fever dream of possibilities. Here, P(A) is not a calculable function but a feeling, a tension, a hunch. It's why we speak of football "moments" rather than strictly of sequences—because in the moment, the game is less a story than it is a field of probabilities unfolding in real time.

To play or watch a game as it happens is to be immersed in emergence. To analyze or narrate it afterward is to impose progression. The two modes don't necessarily contradict one another but rarely align neatly. The backward logic of narration gives us causality; the forward motion of play gives us risk. Emergence is hot, lived time; progression is cool, narrated time.

Football, then, is not just played in 90 minutes. It is played in temporal duality: a chaos of now and an order of after.

GOD MODE

In videogames, "God Mode" is a cheat or developer toggle that removes constraints—invulnerability, infinite resources, perfect execution—so the player can't lose. Uncertainty, risk, and surprise evaporate. If football had a comparable God Mode, matches would become deterministic. Tactics would execute flawlessly, fatigue and injuries wouldn't matter, first touches would never fail, passes would always reach their targets, finishing would be optimal, and refereeing (or VAR) would be error-free. In short, the game would be "solved". Strategy would collapse into a scripted walkthrough, a sure climb to success. Buy three elite forwards and, by design, you win the season. In fact, this was the Paris Saint-Germain recipé from not so long ago. Fortunately, real football resists this. Bounded skill, noise, and contingency keep emergence alive, so the best team doesn't always win, and that's why the sport remains interesting.

Moreover, the God Mode would devalue the very essence of football that fans cherish. It would diminish the excitement surrounding the question of which team is superior, as well as the thrill of tweaking possibilities and contending with the uncertainties of the game. It doesn't sound warm-blooded at all, but as this chapter has shown the game of football plays along these three trajectories:

1. From possibility to probability (increase P to obtain A).
2. From emergence to progression (remove contingency and establish order).
3. From t1 to t2 (find a dominant strategy and a dominant path).

But because football is (still) played by fallible human beings prone to making mistakes, we can never truly know who will dazzle and who will stumble.

NOTES

1 See Norbert Wiener: *Cybernetics: Or Control and Communication in the Animal and the Machine.* MIT Press, 1948.

2 Hans-Joachim Backe: "Narrative Rules? Story Logic and the Structures of Games". *Literary and Linguistic Computing*, 7/3, 2012, p. 244.

3 When Miguel realizes that there is a certain pattern to be followed in how to turn on which switches he has also sparked what could be called *upward causation*: the emergence of a higher entity from a lower one characterized by a causal process leading from the lower level entities to the higher level ones, so that the lower level can be seen as the cause and the higher level as the effect. See Gil Santos: "Upward and Downward Causation from a Relational-Horizontal Ontological Perspective". *Axiomathes*, 25/1, 2015, pp. 23–40.

4 If you really want to dive into the nerdy terrain of mathematical probability spaces, this is the book to read: Athanasios Papoulis: *Probability, Random Values and Stochastic Processes*. McGraw-Hill, 1984.

5 See Aviad Heifetz: *Game Theory*. Cambridge University Press, 2012, for an in-depth study of this (from an economic and management perspective).

6 See Roman Frigg and Stephan Hartmann: "Models in Science". *Stanford Encyclopedia of Philosophy*, 2020. https://plato.stanford.edu/entries/models-science/.

7 See Gerd Gigerenzer: *Rationality for Mortals: How People Cope with Uncertainty*. Oxford University Press. 2008.

8 See Stuart Russell and Peter Norvig: *Artificial Intelligence: A Modern Approach*. Pearson Education Limited, 2016.

9 Jesper Juul: "The Open and the Closed: Games of Emergence and Games of Progression". *Computer Games and Digital Cultures Conference Proceedings*, vol. 1, Tampere University Press, June, 2002.

CHAPTER 7

Games within the Game

Football and Metagaming

When we think about how football is played, we often consider the beauty of individual skills, such as Ronaldo's brilliant dribbling, Haaland's ruthless efficiency, or Mbappé's fierce speed. Some of us take our appreciation a step further and contemplate the beauty of the sport as a result of the tactical setups deployed on the pitch. For some, watching a solid defensive team is incredibly dull. Still, for those interested in the intricacies of collective action, there is beauty in witnessing teams arranged in low blocks,[1] collectively cutting passing lanes while locking down creativity and waiting for the right moment to strike with speed and precision. The French national team under Deschamps exemplifies defensive prowess and technical skill, consistently competing at the highest possible level, not through the brilliant creativity of the players but through the ruthless efficiency of deploying speed in counterattacks.

In this chapter, we explore the relationship between playing by the rules, playing with the rules, and even with the technologies of the game. Game developers and scholars use the concept of metagaming to argue that playing a game is not just about following the rules but also involves playful practices that go beyond traditional ideas of what it means to play. Football serves as a good example for exploring metagaming since some of its rules

DOI: 10.1201/9781003636762-8

are quite open to interpretation. We will use the penalty kick as an example. We will also revisit the offside rule enhanced by video assisted refereeing to demonstrate how the idea of metagaming can deepen our understanding of games and why we play them.

PLAYING WITH AND WITHIN THE RULES

Let's begin with how football is taught. When we examine how football is coached, individual skill and tactical collective action are foundational to our understanding of the game. Coaching youth involves teaching players to develop their technique and game awareness to solve problems on the fly while also understanding each player's different roles on the pitch based on the team's tactical setup.[2] Learning to play football, in the conventional sense, means cultivating technique that serves the team, facilitating both individual and collective problem-solving.

Similarly, when we look at the data revolution in football and how computer models and statistical analysis are becoming more common in understanding the sport, we often focus on studying patterns of play and individual actions as a result of technique or tactical work. Statistics help us measure and understand how a team performs under pressure, when in possession of the ball, and how it builds up play. Likewise, analytical models assist us in recognizing the greatness, potential, or actual ability of any player. We can evaluate how well they have been playing, identify areas for improvement, and determine how they can be stopped.

These perspectives on the game result from how technology has shaped how we spectate and study sports. Football is no different from any other game. We learn the rules through an assemblage of being told what the rules are, and practicing how the rules are applied when we play the game. This includes understanding that we cannot use our hands to touch the ball, the game aims to get the ball across the line inside the goal, and that it is a physical but not intentionally violent sport. Furthermore, we are indoctrinated in the belief that Real Madrid is synonymous with success.[3] Once we gain a basic understanding of the rules, we begin to play, and the practice of action within those rules enhances both our enjoyment of the game and our comprehension of the rules. For instance, we learn technical aspects like how to perform a throw-in correctly, but we also figure out how to exploit the offside rule by timing our runs behind the center backs. The rules transition from mere theory to a practical guide for structuring our actions in the field.

Game studies have developed a way to examine that particular situation, in which players learn the rules and practice by playing. While this idea is at the core of the research field and is present in many academic texts about games, we will explore it using the elegant formulation proposed by Katie Salen and Eric Zimmerman in their book *Rules of Play*.[4] For them, play is "free movement within a more rigid structure" (p. 304). With this expression, these researchers highlight the fundamental back and forth of play and games. Playing is voluntarily submitting oneself to freely accepted, arbitrary rules. Those rules create a space of possibility where players can move with certain degrees of freedom. The pleasure of playing games stems from exploring that freedom and occasionally clashing with the freely accepted boundaries of the experience.[5]

This idea of the back and forth of playing games between rules and free movement, or creativity, is at the core of dominant ideas on aesthetics. The German philosopher Hans-Georg Gadamer[6] wrote about experiencing art as a form of play, in which there is a back and forth of interpretation and emotion between the spectator and the work. That back and forth is key to the aesthetic experience: the beauty of the work of art resides in the way it is experienced as a dialogue between who looks and the work itself. On the other hand, in his landmark work on game aesthetics which we referred to in Chapter 2, Nguyen argues that the voluntary acceptance of rules creates forms of agency that we practice. From that practice, an aesthetic experience emerges. In other words, the beauty of playing a game can be seen as exploring freedom *within* the rigid space of the rules.[7]

We can see that in football. Let's think about what defending means as a way of playing football. And let's be a bit more colloquial for a second. Look, we understand that Bo and I are a bit of an odd couple when it comes to watching football. We are the type that watches a match that ends 0-0, and would have enjoyed every minute of it. We don't claim to be average spectators or argue that the only proper way to enjoy football is to have the kind of geeky, obsessive analysis we dwell over. With this book, we want readers to learn to see and love football not as we do, but as they could, with more knowledge, learning to identify what they enjoy, and with a vocabulary to describe that joy. Let us explain what we look for in a defensive team.

The goal of football is to score more goals than the opponent. Almost all the Laws of the Game are somehow related to this goal: how much time you have to score goals, what is a goal, who and when can score, etc. To achieve this goal, teams ideally attack, and players strive to score as many goals as possible. This can be referred to as the Cruyff school of thought: a 5-4 victory is as valid a result as a 1-0 win, but it brings more excitement. However, there is an alternative perspective on the game that we have discussed in this book regarding Italian and Argentine football. Football can also be viewed as a game won if the opposing team does not score more goals than your team. Instead of relying solely on offensive strategies, the game can be approached by establishing a structure that compels the opponent to make mistakes, preventing them from scoring goals and facilitating the creation of scoring opportunities for our team through counterattacks. Football can become a game of capitalizing on offensive and defensive errors. Accordingly, a team can be trained to induce the other team to make mistakes.

For instance, Deschamp's France employs a physically dominant midfield specializing in high-intensity defensive pressure throughout the match, along with a well-coordinated and solid defensive back line of four players typically positioned no more than 5 to 10 meters from the midfield. France waits for the opponent to advance. When the opponent reaches the French midfield, they face intense physical pressing coordinated between the defense and the midfield. This strategy forces the opposing team to make mistakes, such as misplacing passes. The recoveries of these balls are then used to launch lethal counterattacks, relying on the speed and individual skills of the French forwards.

When we think about the beauty of football, we often focus on the elegance of goals and skills. However, there is also beauty in watching a defensive team play. When a team is reactive, they are trained to understand how another team operates and to neutralize them. This approach represents a way of playing the game, characterized by free movement within a rigid framework. In the case of a clash between an offensive and a reactive team, the beauty lies in how one team focuses on creating a space of possibility, while the other team destroys that space as it is being established. In fact, one beauty of football is this back and forth between creation and destruction of possibility spaces.

But the game doesn't end within the rules. Many aspects can be understood by examining the rules and how teams create possibilities within them.[8] Those moments of generating novel possibilities through the exploration of rules create surprising instances of gameplay. Those moments challenge the very nature of playing the game and the expectations of how it should be played.

Let's illustrate this aspect of the game with an example. The US Women's National Team (USWNT) is one of the greatest women's football teams in history. Their dominance in women's soccer was, for many years, undisputed, shaping the global growth of women's football. Additionally, the USWNT has always been a proud attacking team, relentlessly breaking down opponents with quick plays and physical strength. That's why it was so surprising to see this team, fiercely built around the idea of scoring more goals, waste time in the final minutes of matches during the 2019 World Cup. When they were leading with only a few minutes left, USWNT players would receive the ball and run to the corner to wait, protecting the ball and wasting time until the match ended. It was a frustrating tactic that contradicted the team's history and its dedication to always scoring goals. But, as coach Jill Ellis mentioned, this was a valid tactic within the rules to win the game, and the goal is to win.

This is an intriguing contradiction. According to football rules, the winning team is the one that scores more goals than the opponent after 90 minutes. If we were Johann Cruyff, we'd keep pushing to score until the very last second because that's how we'd win. In reality, most teams play by attacking to score and then, possibly, controlling the game by passing the ball around or setting up a low, defensive line to maintain the lead. What the USWNT did was entirely different. They would get the ball, move toward the opposing team's goal, but instead of trying to score, they would run to the farthest point of the field and wait there. This tactic suggests refusing to truly play the game while still operating within its boundaries, using the space allowed by the rules but intentionally ignoring the spirit of the game. Wasting time is a form of metagaming in football.

THE METAGAME OF A SPORT

Before we explain this perspective, we need to address some academic disclaimers. There is no consensus on the definition of metagaming. Scholars and game developers use the concept in overlapping yet distinct ways.[9] Therefore, we must be specific about what we mean by metagaming in this book. Again, our goal is to introduce and reflect on game studies concepts using football as an example. We are not trying to argue that one specific definition of metagaming is more correct than another. We use those interpretations of the concept that we find productive in explaining football. We will reference other definitions, but these interpretations align better with our goals in this book.

The overall idea of metagame has a debated history. While it's likely that the concept of a "metagame" appeared in mathematical game theory and decision theory, the term as used by game developers and some scholars comes from Richard Garfield's reflections on game design.[10] Since we are writing within the tradition of game studies, we consider Garfield's work the starting point for using this concept. Garfield described metagaming as forms of play "outside" of the game itself.[11]

Now, this way of thinking is problematic: what is inside and outside a game? The ideas that games have both intrinsic and extrinsic elements are confusing.[12] We understand that these distinctions exist, but they become unclear and ineffective when we try to define them. Garfield chose a more general definition, which has become fundamental to understanding metagaming in game studies. The metagame includes what a player brings into the game, takes away from it, what happens between games, and what occurs during a game—not just in terms of playing by the rules, but all the social and material relations that arise while playing. For those interested in Erving Goffman's work,[13] this explanation is similar to how Goffman analyzed games and play: a set of social actions that use a game as a framework and justification.[14]

Let's break down this concept a little. Metagaming refers to activities in play that aren't just about following the rules to reach the goals. In football as a game, the rules create a space and impose physical limits, giving players a clear goal: scoring. When looking at unstructured football play by young children, this basic way of understanding how to play is very clear. Children gather around the ball, don't pass it, and always aim to score. This freeform play is fun and still follows the core rules of the game.

Once children grow up, they begin to see the rules and mechanics of the game not just as strict instructions but as frameworks for action. Improving at playing football involves learning to recognize the space of possibility within the boundaries of the rules. We move from clustering around the ball to spreading out, from always trying to score to passing the ball to teammates in better positions. Playing the game well involves understanding the metagame—how to use the rules to our advantage. As players develop, they understand their roles and start using counter-intuitive moves, like passing the ball backward, which makes the attack more dynamic. Realizing that sometimes the ball needs to go back to the defense to create more space for the offense might seem counter to the original goal of the game as outlined by the rules. Still, this is a form of metagaming.

Garfield would probably dislike this understanding of the concept, as he explicitly defines it as everything that happens outside of the game, or not directly related to playing the game. His strict definition can be trash-talking, the social status acquired from winning a game, or the preparation for playing a game. However, this is precisely the richness of the concept: to play football effectively, it is necessary to prepare, understand the rules as frames and the possibilities they create, and learn how to tune individual and collective skills to achieve the desired playing style. Metagaming happens inside the game, while being played, and outside or around the game, when thinking, writing, and talking about it. Metagaming influences tactics as well. If our team has fast wingers, we could practice a low-block defending structure with fast counter-attacking. If our players are effective with the ball under pressure, we may adopt a possession-based approach, slowly wearing down the opposition through passing and movement. These decisions translate into training patterns internalized as tools for players to use during gameplay. We consider that metagaming, in only a slight perversion of Garfield's original concept.

If we consider Garfield's idea as a starting point, we should recognize that metagaming includes everything that influences how the game is played or experienced. For example, training could be seen as metagaming, since a team prepares to play in a specific way by practicing drills that not only follow the rules but also simulate real game situations, thus avoiding the complexities of actual gameplay. When training to keep possession under pressure, a common exercise involves removing the goals and making the objective to keep the ball for as long as possible, sometimes using a player who can switch between teams. This scenario doesn't happen during actual matches, but it's important to practice the skill of maintaining ball possession under pressure. The design and practice of such exercises represent a form of metagaming, an interface with the game beyond itself, as Garfield would put it.

In this sense, metagaming can also explain how professional coaches utilize press conferences to influence the flow of a match. The Portuguese coach José Mourinho was a master of manipulating the press conference as part of the game, discussing referees, the opponent, and the press itself to create a mood and vibe that could affect the team's performance.

This use of metagaming, defined as anything outside the game rules and gameplay that influences how the game is played or experienced, is incredibly helpful in explaining why football is more than just 90 minutes on a field. In reality, no game is played solely within the boundaries of the rules regarding time and space. Like all social and cultural activities, games extend beyond the gameplay itself, affecting everyday life and shaping how play is observed before and after the event. The popularity of football can be viewed through this perspective. The different metagames associated with the sport—from hooligans to collectible cards to video games—all contribute to the environment of the sport's experience. As the sport's influence grows, it becomes linked with politics, making phenomena like sportswashing part of the larger metagame. The worldwide impact of the game is reflected in how enjoyable it is to engage in the metagame of football from a distance, without actually playing the sport.

However, if we apply this concept too broadly, it may become too vague in its use. Metagaming can be seen, as we have just shown, as a broad category that describes how various factors surrounding football influence the experiences of players, coaches, clubs, fans, and nation-states. At the same time, metagaming is also used as a more specific and concrete idea, often in competitive gaming, to describe players' behaviors within games. In the following section, we will clarify other usages of the metagame concept.

WHAT WE TALK ABOUT WHEN WE TALK ABOUT METAGAMING (AND FOOTBALL)

In the context of competitive or professional gameplay in collective card games, board games, or video games, the *term* "meta" is often used to describe how highly skilled players identify dominant strategies that enhance their chances of winning. The classic application of this concept pertains to the various openings that a competitive chess player can employ. By selecting a particular opening, a chess player engages in a *meta*—an approach that evolves into a series of actions designed to provide a winning advantage against an opponent. When the opponent recognizes that *meta*, they will implement an opposing *strategy* to counter the advantages of that sequence of actions.

This use of *metagaming* might be confusing if we relate it to concepts such as strategies and tactics. There is a semantic overlap between strategies and *meta* in competitive games. Therefore, we should strive to provide working definitions of these concepts to understand better how we can apply them to games, from chess and *Starcraft* to football. We will use football as a reference for these definitions and draw on philosopher Michel De Certeau for the definitions of tactics and strategies.[15]

In this book, we define a strategy as selecting a specific, well-defined method to narrow down the possibilities and achieve the game's goal. This strategy involves a series of mechanics and interpretations of rules as procedures to follow in order to win according to the game's rules. Strategies are usually planned in advance and implemented at the start of a gameplay session, which limits the player's ability to explore different options. In De Certeau, strategy functions as a way for power to manifest itself by creating an order that influences people's agency. In our view, a strategy establishes game elements that initially restrict agency in ways that help secure victory. A player will decide or be guided on which strategy to use before beginning the game. Game designers test various strategies within the game to ensure variety in conflict and to keep the game enjoyable by encouraging different strategic choices.

If we apply our understanding of strategies to football, we start by recognizing that the team's formation on the field is the first step in the strategy. Whether a team chooses a 4-4-2, a 3-5-2-1, or a 4-3-3, all these formations are already implementing certain strategies. It's important to understand that this setup is not as crucial as some might think, especially if we follow certain football pundits who focus on these numbers. This initial arrangement of players on the field is just the first phase of the strategic process. It's similar to the placement of pieces on a chessboard or, more accurately, the setup of a deck in a collective card game. While it is important and deserves attention, it is only the beginning of strategic action and doesn't determine how a team actually plays.

To understand how a team plays, we need to examine the strategies used in their initial positioning. To make this clearer, we can look at two historical examples. José Mourinho's Chelsea in the early 2000s was one of the top defensive teams ever. Using a 4-2-3-1 formation, Chelsea was relentless in breaking down the opponent's game. The key players were the two holding midfielders (the "2" in the formation), whose job was not to create plays but to prevent the opposition from building attacks, whether through counter-attacks or controlling the midfield via passing. Prioritizing athletic ability over technical skill, Mourinho built barriers in the midfield by closely connecting the center backs and these defensive midfielders. To score goals, Mourinho relied on a strong striker, the legendary Didier Drogba, who combined technique and strength to make long balls into the box more effective. The wingbacks and offensive wide players aimed to get the ball into the box quickly, trying to disrupt the opponent's defensive structure through fast plays and physical dominance. However, Mourinho recognized the importance of creativity and always included a skilled number 10 who could dictate the game from a position ahead of the defensive midfielders. Mourinho's Chelsea aligned players in a 4-2-3-1 formation, but the main strategy was to control the game through physical play and direct, straightforward attacks toward the goal. All player movements, positions, and actions supported this approach, from the deep runs of the wide attackers to the numerous crosses from the wingbacks.

This was a strategy that led to success. But what happens when a strategy does not work? The other example we want to highlight is the Spanish men's National Team's unsuccessful passing and controlling strategy in their 2022 World Cup match against Morocco. Before we continue, it is worth mentioning that the Spanish national coach at the time, Luis Enrique, is one of the most innovative coaches of the modern era, and that his strategic choices, particularly in squad selection, were excellent. Furthermore, Spain was occasionally unlucky in that match when we look at the statistics of the game. Spain lost, but that match's margin between success and failure was unusually narrow, even for elite football games.

That match is relatively well known because some heralded it as the end of the Spanish strategy of tiki-taka, which involves winning the game through short cumulative passes intended to keep the ball away from the opponent while trying to force them into an error. This type of possession game is an old concept, likely originating with the Hungarian national team of the 1950s and further developed by the Dutch school of Rinus Michels and Johan Cruyff, as we discussed in Chapter 5. Its logic is simple: pass the ball continuously so the other team cannot score because they don't have it. Through fast passing, the opposing team will eventually make a mistake and disorganize themselves, allowing a goal to be scored. While this strategy is often characterized as an offensive approach to football, that is not entirely accurate. In fact, this possession game is a very defensive strategy, as it prefers to avoid risks by passing rather than opening up to fast transitions. We may remember Johan Cruyff's or Pep Guardiola's FC Barcelona teams as the heralds of this possession play. Still, when looking back at how these teams actually played, it is worth noting that possession always led to fast movement of the forwards, with wingers constantly making runs off the ball without hope of receiving a pass to disorganize the opposing team. FC Barcelona passed the ball to control the game and to win. Still, the passes were only part of a complicated strategy involving movements off the ball to allow the play to progress and for decisive players to receive a pass in the most favorable way possible.

If we analyze the Spanish team's implementation of this strategy, we can see two distinct approaches. On the one side, there's the offensive, movement-off-the-ball style exemplified by the national team that won the EuroCup in 2012. That team resembled FC Barcelona most, with players constantly moving to create spaces accessed through controlled passing. On the other side, the Spanish National Team that triumphed in the 2010 World Cup demonstrated a more defensive take on this strategy. This team succeeded by scoring only eight goals and winning matches by a one-goal margin, except against the underdog Honduras. Although the victory was deserved, it raises the question of whether that interpretation of the possession strategy was genuinely offensive or simply a form of passive defense.

In any case, this strategy of passing to maintain control of the game came to an end as a popular coaching method for the Spanish National Team during the 2022 World Cup, after their failure to defeat Morocco in the quarterfinals. Spain completed 1019 passes but managed only three shots on goal and did not score any. The team selection suited this approach, including defensive midfielder and Ballon d'Or winner Rodri playing as a center back, to ensure passing originated from the defensive line. The problem with that Spanish strategy was that Morocco effectively closed the passing lanes and marked the runners, which gradually forced the Spanish team to rely on passing without making deep runs off the ball. This strategy failed not because they lacked the right players, but because it was not fully executed, missing the deep runs off the ball that generate the movement needed for offensive passing. Strategies are complex systems, and when one element fails, the entire strategy can break down.

The concept of tactics can explain why Spain's strategy failed. According to De Certau, tactics are actions that can never be as dominant as a strategy. They are actions that undermine strategies by finding spaces that allow for opposition. De Certeau's work provides a basis for political interpretation; however, in our case, we will use the concept to describe the specific actions taken during a game to prevent the success of a strategy. Tactics involve responding to strategic patterns as a way of countering them. For example, when Morocco faced Spain, the team used a defensive tactical approach that allowed runners to move freely without being tracked, while focusing on cutting off passing lanes. If the runs failed to create chaos in the defensive line, then passing was just passing and not threatening. The tactic worked, and Spain lost in a penalty shootout.

This understanding of tactics can also explain offensive patterns. Teams have offensive and defensive strategies, and the roles of coaches and players are to develop tactics that can dismantle strategic setups. A good example of offensive tactics is playing the third man. If we return to Michels and Cruyff's concepts of offensive football, we can see that players need to be in constant movement for their systems to function. One of these movement patterns is playing the third man. Let's explain this tactic in detail. Typically, when considering passing in football, we view it as a movement that involves the passer and the receiver. A player passes, another receives. Conventional wisdom dictates that the second players pass the ball, they should move to a slightly new position to create new pockets of space.

But passing can involve more than two players. For example, if a midfielder passes to a winger, the wingback immediately starts a run to overlap the winger. In contrast, the midfielder moves into a pocket of space ahead. If this is a third-man play, the winger should pass to the overlapping wingback and then move toward the box to receive a return pass from the winger. In other words, the pass from the midfielder to the winger was actually a delayed pass to the wingback, who is the third man in this combination.

Playing the third man is a passing tactic often used to break down low defensive blocks by exploiting off-the-ball movements that are frequently overlooked individually by the defense. By practicing these deferred passing strategies, teams that employ this style of attacking football can create danger not by positioning players in threatening zones, but by having them arrive in those dangerous areas. It becomes a way of playing football that triggers a desired future state several steps ahead.

In summary, we now have three concepts to understand gameplay behavior. Strategies determine how teams or players generally play. Tactics describe specific actions within those strategies aimed at either winning or countering an opposing strategy. Metagaming includes anything outside the game that influences it and refers to strategies that are formalized and widely recognized by a community.

All of these are examples of strategies, tactics, and metagaming that operate within the rules. They are applications of concepts explaining how players and coaches act within the goals set by the game's rules. However, the depth of the metagaming concept lets us describe actions that don't follow the rules but instead manipulate the rules to gain specific tactical advantages in the game.

Let's revisit the initial examples in this chapter. When the USWNT defended their winning record in a World Cup match by not occupying a corner of the pitch, they were adhering to a traditional metagaming strategy in football: wasting time. Since football doesn't track time with a stopwatch, teams have developed ways over the years to spend minutes doing nothing related to the actual goals, hoping the referee won't account for those lost seconds or minutes in extra time. This is classic metagaming: analyzing a specific set of rules and finding ways to exploit them for an advantage. In this case, it's exploiting the lack of a stopwatch and the rule that extra time is a subjective call made by the referee.

In the case of the USWNT, their metagaming essentially identified that while the rules of the game encourage teams to score more goals, they say nothing about playing without the intention to score. Therefore, taking the ball and going to a corner to wait for the clock to run out is just as valid a strategy as always trying to score goals. It may be boring or tiptoe the line of appropriate sportsmanship, but it's an effective way to secure a positive outcome in the context of high-stakes professional play.

In this example, metagaming refers to a form of play that explores bending the rules. That is, interpreting rules in creative ways so that novel strategies and tactics can be employed to win the game. Essentially, this type of metagaming identifies combinations of rules that allow alternative paths to achieving the game's goal, for example, by permitting novel strategic or tactical approaches. This meta encourages creative interpretation but sometimes interferes with the culture of the sport or the general understanding of what it means to play a game. However, it is never illegal or against the rules of the game. It is a matter of viewing the rules as freely accepted boundaries that can be nudged, if not outright moved, to create novel possibilities.

Wasting time is quite negative, as many football fans dislike teams that use this approach to hold onto a match's result. In simple terms, it's an unattractive tactic. However, metagaming can sometimes lead to interesting strategies within the game. During the 2024–2025 season, coach Hansi Flick's FC Barcelona exceeded expectations by combining the classic Spanish passing style with a German high-press, high-intensity approach. Yet, that team started the season by playing in a way made possible through metagaming. As mentioned earlier in the book, Flick's Barça used a very high defensive line aimed at catching opponents offside. This defensive tactic required great coordination among the back four, but it also depended on the Spanish league's innovative use of automatic VAR.

During that season, La Liga introduced a system equipped with numerous cameras designed to create a 3D image of the game whenever offside was uncertain. This system allowed for the evaluation of marginal offsides that human referees might not accurately judge. As a result, with proper coordination of the defensive line, it became possible to maintain a high defensive line with less fear of mistakes, since all plays would be automatically reviewed by VAR, and any goals would be disallowed if there was even a slight offside. FC Barcelona had a strong start to the 2024–2025 season, taking advantage of this metagaming approach, which also pressured other teams to find ways to counter this tactical defensive strategy. Over time, opposing teams learned to position runners from the second line to exploit long passes that shifted play from one side of the pitch to another, making FC Barcelona less dependent on their high line due to this counterstrategy.

What matters about this offside example is that it illustrates an instance of metagaming that considers both the material and technical implementation of rules in play, as well as how these conditions can be manipulated to create new ways of playing. By examining not only the rules of the game but also how they are executed on the pitch through technological means that minimize ambiguity and interpretation, the 2024–2025 FC Barcelona displayed a creative approach to playing, a form of inventive metagaming.

THE GAME, GAMED

In this chapter, we explored three key concepts in game studies that can enhance the study of football. We primarily focus on the concept of metagaming. There are two main ways to understand metagaming: one refers to all elements external to the game-as-object that influence how the game is played in a particular session. The second understanding of metagaming describes ways of playing the game *within* or in accordance *with* the rules. By game-as-object, we refer to the combination of rules and material conditions that define a game, from the ball to the Laws of the Game. Metagaming can describe home-pitch advantage, the use of media by clubs before and after the match, or any other instance of play outside the prescribed rules during the match.

Viewing metagaming as playing *within* the rules highlights the distinction between strategies and tactics. Strategies are forms of structuring play that provide overall approaches to achieving the game's goals by adhering to the rules in specific ways. A strategy formalizes the attempt to create a beneficial possibility space that can lead to victory. A tactic is a specific response to a strategy aimed at breaking or exploiting the possibility spaces established by the opposing team's strategic arrangement. Football can be seen as a game where teams are coached on strategic concepts, which are then put into action during play through tactical decisions and patterns.

At the same time, metagaming can describe forms of playing games that involve manipulating the rules—not illegally, but bending their interpretation to create advantageous ways of achieving the game's goals. Game rules can be ambiguous, and while there is a cultural and social consensus on how to follow them, their ambiguity can inspire creativity and improvisation. In these pockets of creativity, metagaming becomes a means of discovering advantages that can lead to winning the game. Playing with the rules may seem controversial, but it represents a type of play that acknowledges that games are artificial constructs of freely accepted rules, and that as long as those rules are not explicitly broken, all forms of expression that they permit are valid forms of playing the game. Even if that means wasting time in a corner.

While this chapter has examined specific ways of understanding concepts to help game studies scholars analyze sports similarly to other games, it also has a different goal—our own form of metagaming. Recently, the conversation around football has become more intricate. Journalists and writers have created a rich vocabulary to describe the game, and newspapers and publishers have benefited from this increase in game literacy. Our aim is to boost this literacy by showing how the idea of metagaming can help start discussions and thoughts about aspects of playing that are often hard to defend. Is a team's delay tactics ethical or unethical? Is attacking football morally better than defensive football? While we don't expect writers and journalists to accept these ideas fully, we hope they can help organize their thoughts and communicate why the sport's beauty and cultural importance go beyond just scoring goals or building large stadiums; it is deeper, in how it connects communities, perspectives, and practices, reflecting the multiple dimensions of beauty and fun that make the sport enjoyable overall.

NOTES

1 A "low block" is a way of defining a team that seats deep defensively, cedes initiative to their opponents, and tries to achieve goals by counter-attacking. "Mid block" teams are more balanced and capable of switching tactics, while "high block" teams often make use of the offside trap to try to play for as long as they can on the opposing team's side.
2 Wein, 2007.
3 We are joking, of course. Everybody knows that football is a game of 11 against 11, and Germany always wins. Real Madrid has nothing on the German national team.
4 Salen and Zimmerman, 2003.
5 Elsewhere in this book these ideas are discussed from the perspective of the aesthetics of play (Nguyen, 2020), and play theory (Suits, 1978). Since we don't want to repeat the same references over and over again, we urge the reader to read the chapter on the offside rule for a more detailed reflection on this understanding of playing games and the pleasure of submitting oneself to rules.
6 Gadamer, 2004.
7 See our chapter on possibility spaces for a more in-depth discussion of these ideas.
8 In fact, a key theme in this book is to illustrate the vocabulary that game studies has developed to analyze the creation, experience, and social and cultural impact of these possibility spaces.
9 Carter et al., 2012.
10 Elias et al., 2012.
11 Sicart, 2015.
12 Consalvo, 2009.
13 Goffman, 1961.
14 Stenros, 2015.
15 De Certau's work falls on the intersection of political philosophy and anthropology. In our text we will not be making a political reflection, but we will take the concepts from a more theoretical perspective. We will leave for future research the reflection on whether teams that deploy certain tactics or strategies are reflecting certain politics.

CHAPTER 8

Dark Play

AT THE CITY ZOO, four pygmy monkeys spill into a sandy enclosure that might as well be a pitch. A bruised banana becomes the ball. The low curb reads like a touchline; the climbing posts suggest goal frames; shaded corners double as dugouts. The game begins in a flurry. There are feints, tumbles, and darts. Two monkeys hurl themselves into the chase, tails flagging, faces open, bodies shaking with obvious delight. A third hangs back, spooked by the jostle, skittering to the edge and then to the safety of a mother's chest. A minute later, reassured, it whizzes back to make a desperate toe-prod at the banana. The fourth hovers between roles—sometimes playmaker, sometimes spoiler—testing how far one can tug an ear or pull a tail before the squeak changes key. Roughness flashes, a shove too hard, a nip too sharp, yet the group resets with tiny rituals. Then, a pause, a sideways bounce, and a lowered head that seems to say, *this is play*. It is for fun, and it is, in that primate way, also dead serious.

We will return to these monkeys. For now, hold the image of a tiny society that keeps its game alive by maintaining a shared frame—a social contract that permits mock aggression while forestalling real harm. In this sense, the monkeys are role models for fandom: when the frame holds, there is joy; when it breaks, there is pain.

DOI: 10.1201/9781003636762-9

Football, too, has its aesthetic dimension. The beautiful game is often described in terms of flair, rhythm, flow, and grace. It is celebrated for its creativity and capacity to surprise. But just as aesthetic structures can become instruments of territorial control, so too can playfulness turn. It can mutate. What begins as joy may veer into aggression, into transgression, into subversion. The frisky impulse does not always result in benevolent forms of sociality. Sometimes, it descends into what we might call *dark play*.

This chapter follows football fandom and its evolution from light to dark, from liberating play to corrosive forms of gaming. We look at football fan culture not only as a site of celebration and belonging, but also as a theatre of tribalism and violence. We consider how rituals of spectatorship intersect with subcultures that weaponize play for destructive ends, and we begin in the exact counter image to such ruin, in the German town Hamburg.

ST. PAULI

The sun dips below the horizon and casts an amber glow across Hamburg. The St. Pauli Stadium stands amidst the bohemian neighborhood that surrounds it. The blast of a vuvuzela fills the atmosphere as crowds of supporters adorned in the brown and white jerseys of FC St. Pauli flock the streets and shops. It is match night.

Quaint cafes with outdoor seating spill over onto the bustling sidewalks, where artists and musicians find solace in their creativity, their works garnishing the walls with wild colors and messages. The scent of street food wafts through the air, competing with the whiffs of outlandish spices from the multicultural restaurants that dot the avenues. The people of St. Pauli are a living testament to diversity, and as the game approaches, the energy intensifies. As locals and visitors intermingle, one begins to question if the St. Pauli Stadion, with its history and fanbase, is more than just a sporting venue. Maybe it is a sanctuary for those who seek refuge from the checks and balances of the ordinary. It represents a microcosm of the world of sports fandom that defies convention and instead champions the principles of inclusion, diversity, and standing up against injustice.[1]

Inside the neighborhood of St. Pauli, the stadium is a place where individuals of all backgrounds are embraced, where the power of unity prevails over division, and where the game might become a catalyst for change.

Perhaps to remind the world that football is and never was not just a game, but a force that can reshape communities and inspire the human spirit.

It was around the mid-1980s that the club's cult aura began to shine. In this period, a group known as the "Black Block" congregated on the terraces behind the dugouts of the Millerntor Stadium. The ever-growing crowd drew from alternative subcultures, and the club quickly gained a reputation as the football home for those without a home in football. Their anti-establishment romanticism became evident after the pirate skull-and-crossbones became their defining symbol (see Figure 8.1). A man known as "Doc Mabuse", referencing the 1922 movie *Dr. Mabuse the Gambler*, directed by Fritz Lang, first brought the flag to the stadium.

FIGURE 8.1 The St. Pauli flag.

At the time, Doc Mabuse lived in a nomadic commune with 40 other squatters who identified as punks. Such a combination was a common sight at the Millerntor and naturally fostered empathy with the poor and the downtrodden.

Nowadays, St. Pauli hosts an annual wheelchair football tournament. They aid the homeless and asylum seekers in Hamburg in the shape of

The St. Pauli Refugee Team. They participate in the annual Hamburg Pride Parade. There is something about football, whether it be the culture, history, or social fabric of fandom, that hovers between enthusiasm and destruction, between the vivacity of play and the toxicity of domination. Why does the culture of football induce both violence and wonder?[2]

"REAL MEN"

The civic gestures of St. Pauli mark one pole of football culture. At the other lies a harder edge where belonging curdles into boundary-making. It is this edge, from classic hooliganism to contemporary forms of "casual" violence, that the next pages confront.

The history of hooliganism can be traced back to the early 20th century in England. However, it was during the 1960s and 1970s that hooliganism began to gain notoriety due to the rise of football-related violence and clashes between rival groups of fans.[3] There are many reasons for the emergence of hooliganism. Some of them include social and economic factors, territorial conflicts between fan groups, excessive alcohol consumption, and the desire for dominance and power among certain blocs of fans. Hooliganism often arises from a sense of identity and belonging to a specific team or club, leading to confrontations with rival fans. This phenomenon is known as neo-tribalism.[4]

In the 1980s, hooliganism reached its peak in English football, with incidents of mass violence, pitch invasions, and severe clashes between rival fan groups. One of the most notorious tragedies occurred in 1985 during the Heysel Stadium disaster in Brussels, Belgium. A rattle between Liverpool and Juventus fans resulted in the death of 39 people, leading to a ban on English clubs from participating in European competitions for several years.

One specific subculture within football hooliganism is known as "casuals". Casuals emerged in the 1970s and 1980s in the United Kingdom, especially in Liverpool and Manchester, and developed a recognizable fashion style and subcultural identity. They were characterized by their preference for designer clothing, often associated with football "firms" led by a "top boy".[5] Casuals adopted a different approach compared to traditional hooligan groups. Instead of wearing conventional club colors, they favored expensive clothing brands, such as Stone Island, Lacoste, and Aquascutum. This change in attire allowed them to blend into crowds and evade police attention. The casuals' emphasis on fashion, music, and a specific lifestyle made it more appealing to younger fans.

To be a hooligan is to live a tribal lifestyle. It is full of subcultural chumminess, and it is portrayed in British movies such as *Football Factory* (2004), *Green Street Hooligans* (2005), and *The Firm* (2009), among others.[6] When the films came out they were seen as representations of debauched youngsters and the "good old ultra-violence", echoing the words of Alex, the protagonist of Anthony Burgess' novel *A Clockwork Orange* from 1962. But they also served as a recruitment campaign, bringing fans together in search of camaraderie and purpose. As Matt, portrayed by Elijah Wood, admits after a brawl in *Green Street*: "It's so much easier to make friends when you realize you're not made of glass".

While casual fans may have appeared less confrontational than traditional hooligans, they were still involved in ferocious clashes with rival groups. They often organized prearranged fights known as "meetings" away from stadiums or orchestrated confrontations on match days. The infamous 1985 FA Cup tie at Kenilworth Road between Luton Town and Millwall resulted in a staggering 81 reported injuries. Another intense rivalry is the Old Firm Derby between Glasgow-based clubs Rangers and Celtic. "The Green Street Boys" took their name from Green Street in the London Borough of Newham, the former location of West Ham's home stadium, Upton Park. "The Boys" harbor a particular hatred for Millwall, a mere four miles away, separated by the River Thames.

The 2016 European Football Championship saw an explosion of violence in Marseille, Southern France, covered by both traditional and social media. Accompanied by stripped-down funk music, members of Russian hooligan groups, trained in military tactics, displayed guerrilla-like precision in confronting their beer-drinking, soft-bellied English counterparts. These confrontations were recorded on GoPro cameras and shared on YouTube. The scenes are unsettling, particularly one of a British senior citizen enduring a violent blow to the head with what appears to be a hammer. The nature of the footage was further amplified by the connection between the upbeat music and the phenomenon known in Russia as *voinushka*, "the little war". The Russian football fighters were bored; they needed a little war to entertain themselves. Following the unrest in Marseille, a spokesperson from the Russian Secret Service named Vladimir Markin stated that European police were simply unaccustomed to "encountering real men" and that the West, in general, had grown too accustomed to "men only participating in gay parades". Dark play, it seems, was simply the norm among those craving for a little war.

APPROPRIATION

Playfulness is often mistaken for frivolity. In everyday speech, to call something "playful" is to suggest lightness, perhaps even triviality, a lack of seriousness. But as scholars of play have long insisted, play is never simply about diversion. It is a potent cultural force, an expressive mode, and a tool for critique, resistance, and appropriation.

Miguel Sicart holds that playfulness is not a thing but a way of being in the world. It is a mode of engagement, situational, tactical, and often subversive. In *Play Matters* (2014) he writes that playfulness is an attitude we can take toward spaces, people, and objects. This attitude allows us to reframe the world, to see its elements not as fixed or instrumental but as pliable, reconfigurable, and open to reinterpretation. A stone can be a ball. A street corner can be a goalpost. A chant in the stands can morph into a coded message, layered with meaning.

Play is thus not confined to designated spaces or structured activities. It is *appropriative* by nature. To play is to claim a right to intervene in the normative use of things, spaces, and behaviors. Sicart argues that playfulness is inherently political in this sense. It is a way of appropriating the world that resists dominant logics. In this sense, play possesses the capacity to invert the structures and norms we take for granted—or more generally the rules of social life—and instead use them, in play, as canvases for vibrancy. Hence, a designated playground is not needed for play to emerge. A protest can be playful. A prank can be political. A stadium, intended for orderly entertainment, can become a site of ritualized chaos.

Appropriation is not about ownership in the capitalist or legal sense, but about usage, to reclaim the right to reinterpret or repurpose. This has enormous implications for how we think about sports spectatorship and fan culture. For example, when fans rewrite chants, choreograph illegal pyrotechnics, or sneak contraband banners into tightly surveilled stadiums, they are engaging in playful acts of resistance. They are reimagining what the football spectacle is, and whom it belongs to.

But appropriation is double-edged. Playful appropriation can easily slide into dominative behavior. What is liberating for one group can be oppressive or exclusionary for another. The same tactics that allow playful protest—masking identity, bending rules, reconfiguring spaces—can also enable aggression, harassment, and the symbolic reassertion of power. This is where the line between playfulness and dark play begins to blur.

Take, for example, the now-familiar sight of flares and smoke bombs in *ultra* football culture. Ultras are highly organized supporter groups known for relentless, coordinated support. They chant, build giant tifos, drum, and deploy pyrotechnics guided by strict group codes and identity. Unlike hooligans whose focus is fighting, ultras center on spectacle and loyalty. For the ultras in Spain, Italy, Greece, and South America, these are not simply tools of spectacle but acts of defiance, appropriations of stadium space against the sanitizing forces of corporate football. Yet, these same appropriative gestures can also feed exclusionary, even violent group identities. The chant becomes a weapon. The terrace becomes a battlefield. The space meant for joy and community building becomes one of intimidation, toxicity, and aggression.

The notion of playfulness as appropriation reveals its latent volatility. It is a way of taking hold of the world, but what one does with that grip is not predetermined. Appropriation sometimes opens room for inclusivity, criticality, and joyful rupture. Think of St. Pauli. In others, it shores up hostility and deeply entrenched hierarchies. This ambiguity is vital to understanding the kinds of playfulness we see in contemporary football fandom.

Perhaps this is why we shouldn't romanticize play. Its creative and rebellious potential does not guarantee good ethical outcomes all the time. Playfulness can be misused, just as beauty can be instrumentalized, and governmental infrastructure can be repressive. The power to reimagine is also the power to distort, exclude, or harm. It is precisely because playfulness is a *power*, an ability to reshape and appropriate the world, that we must approach it with both appreciation and caution. In this light, playfulness is not simply the opposite of seriousness, nor is it necessarily virtuous. It is a form of agency that can just as easily illuminate as obscure, connect as divide, liberate as oppress.

WHY SO SERIOUS?

"Why so serious?", asks the Joker (Heath Ledger) in Christopher Nolan's *The Dark Knight* (2008). It is a line delivered in the context of a villain's anarchic philosophy, but it also speaks to the tension between playfulness and its dangerous flipside: dark play.

Play appears to be a trivial matter, a pursuit of joy and impulsiveness. It is an expression of freedom, a break from the rigid confines of responsibility. However, as the late English philosopher Gregory Bateson's work on the nature of play suggests, the boundary between play and seriousness is much thinner and more complex than it seems. In his foundational essay "A Theory of Play and Fantasy" (1972) Bateson draws attention to the faint distinction between play and reality, particularly through the behavior of monkeys in social settings.[7] Just like our opening example, he famously observed that monkeys communicate through play by adopting different frames of behavior: one that signals that the actions are "serious" and another that signals they are "playful". This duality allows monkeys to engage in rough and sometimes painful behavior (like mock fighting) without crossing the line into actual aggression. The play frame sets up a special condition that strengthens the social bond enough to endure even the physical jaggedness of play. Play can hurt, but the rule of the game is that it is not truly harmful.

The idea that play can involve a certain hurt is important. The Joker's mockery is not just for amusement; it is designed to provoke discomfort. It's not about being serious in the conventional sense, but it's about creating dissonance between appearance and intention. This duality between pain and pleasure, seriousness and play, is what makes dark play so potent and dangerous. Just as Bateson noted in his study of animal play, the problem arises when those lines blur, when the frame of play gets broken, and the playful becomes serious in a way that causes harm—*did we agree on this?* The Joker's unruly nature is a prime example of how playfulness, unshackled from any rules or frames, can quickly slip into destruction. In *The Dark Knight*, the Joker's antics are played off as a joke, but his actions, like blowing up a hospital or threatening the city, are deadly serious (even though Ledger sometimes portrays them as everyday routine, which makes them even more disturbing). His entire worldview is built on the idea that the thin line separating play and bellicosity can be erased, and that laughter and destruction can coexist in a surreal, unnerving harmony.

While Bateson's monkeys signaled play through body language and behavior, thereby allowing violence without actual harm, the Joker rejects these social frames entirely. He is the Batesonian anti-monkey. He performs a form of play that has no boundaries and inflicts harm under the guise of freedom. It is a profound critique of what happens when play loses its ethical frame and becomes a tool for manipulation and terror.

Among football ultras aggression and passion for a team are celebrated in equal measure. On the terraces, they blur the line between cheerleading for their team and unleashing an organized storm of violence against rival supporters. Their chants, often full of braggadocio and defiance, operate within a structure of play: the rules of the terraces dictate what's acceptable and what's not. Yet, when rivalries escalate, the violent acts committed under the guise of play become serious. The idea that football fans can get away with acts of violence because it is seen as part of the game speaks to the way play's moral boundaries become weak in certain social contexts. What is framed as "banter" or "lads being lads" can, in truth, be deeply demeaning and aggressive. The monkeys that Bateson wrote about were innocent in the sense that they allowed joy and aggression to coexist. Ultras veil the seriousness of their mayhem in playful appearance.

Bateson points out that playful communication requires an understanding that signals "this is play". Without this shared understanding, the line between playful and serious action becomes impossible to discern. In hooligan culture, play is not a simple act of enjoyment; it is embedded in a larger narrative of violence and resistance. The line between playful rivalry and serious violence becomes invisible, especially when the players and the fans are so immersed in the culture. The group dynamics of football fans amplify this dynamic, turning what could have been an inoffensive moment of fun into an act of ritualized destruction.

The game that hooligans play is one of physical dominance and territoriality, but it operates under a perverse logic that allows them to justify their violent actions as part of the spectacle of football. They are football fans, not fans of violence. The rhetoric of "we're just having fun" or "it's part of the game" echoes the same ideology of the Joker, where bedlam and demolition are cloaked in the guise of liberation and playful spontaneity. Here, the distinction between serious violence and playful banter is eroded, and we are left with a sociocultural practice that thrives on aggression masked as joy.

Bateson's ideas on play suggest that the ability to distinguish between play and seriousness is not only a cognitive skill, but also a social construct. Play, he argues, is an inherently social act that depends on an established social order to function. This means that in contexts where social structures are weak or chaotic—like those in certain extreme fan cultures—the boundaries of play can be easily manipulated.

What becomes clear is that the ability to play, and to signal the boundaries between play and seriousness, is itself a form of power. The Joker understands this intimately. His entire thinking is built around the idea that power can be wielded by destabilizing the frame of play, allowing chaos to seep into every aspect of life. His line "Why so serious?" becomes a challenge to those who think they can contain the chaos of play within civilized norms. By tearing down these frames, he exposes the fragility of order and the violence lurking beneath the surface of the so-called serious.

The same logic can be applied to the fan violence in football. At its best, football is a game of team spirit, creativity, and joy; qualities that align with play's most positive aspects. However, in many contexts, the game becomes about the collective exertion of power. The boundary between what's playful and what's serious collapses when fans, much like the Joker, engage in destruction while simultaneously claiming the mantle of liberation. They take the structures of football, its rituals, its rules, and use them to justify violence. In doing so, they shift the meaning of the game from a collective expression of elation to a battleground of power, identity, and exclusion.

WHEN IN ROME

Play involves a negotiation of boundaries, a careful calibration of what is allowed and what is forbidden, Brian Sutton-Smith writes in *The Ambiguity of Play* (1997). However, the rules governing play are often ambiguous, flexible, or susceptible to manipulation. It is in this ambiguity that dark play thrives, where individuals or groups push or even break these boundaries in pursuit of power and dominance over others.

Two of Italy's most politically charged football clubs are Lazio and Roma, both residing in Rome. Known as the *Derby della Capitale*, their rivalry is one of the fiercest in Europe, and the relationship between the two clubs is fraught with historical and political tensions. For Lazio and Roma ultras the game is not simply about who scores more goals; it's about representing their group, exerting power, and making a statement against the other. The violence that erupts during these derbies is not just incidental but is embedded in the ritualistic and performative aspects of the game. During the 2019 Derby of the Capital, among many other, violence spilled over into the streets long before the match even began.

For football lovers what is most disturbing, in fact, is that the match itself is secondary to the group dynamics at play. The Lazio supporters were just waiting to sneak in on their Roma counterparts, the same way that Russian hooligans dressed to the occasion as urban guerilla fighters snapped into a military campaign in the streets of Marseille in 2016 that caught the English fans by surprise. The football match itself is framed—or hijacked—as a performance of collective strength, with the ultimate goal not being the scoreline on the board but the ability to demonstrate power over the other group. The rituals of fan behavior, the chanting, organizing, and attacking, are used to assert dominance and to perform group identity through violence.

For the Western media and public anno 2016, this mood of bellicose jingoism made in Russia was morally too much. And though he did not use those exact words, Vladimir Markin from the Russian Secret Service might as well have responded: "Why so serious?"

LESSONS FROM JERUSALEM

Very often violent fans yearn for a time when football was inherently battle-ready and had not yet been domesticated. Stern hooligans hate modern stadium seating, family friendly regulations, and woke culture in the style of St. Pauli. The most obsessive among them care more about their sphere of violence than the actual match and its progress. Very often they do not even watch the game too busy shouting commands and shepherding the shared singing on the stadium terraces. They cling to this sphere, seemingly finding some strange comfort in the rituals of dark play, even when there are no longer any political, social, or religious reasons for it, like there once were in Belfast, Rome or Madrid. Why?

Because the theatre is the point. The choreography of the curva, the march to the ground, the flag ceremony, the capo's call-and-response on a perch with his back turned to the pitch—these are stages, scripts, cues. In many ultra ends, like "The Kop", at Anfield, home to Liverpool FC, or "Fondo Sur", at Real Madrid's Bernabéu stadion, the unwritten rule is precisely not to watch the game. You conduct it. You time the flare to the 13th minute. You keep the line tight when the banner drops. You scan for away fans drifting off their column. Spectatorship becomes craft, a second-order game that aims to maintain the performance of belonging. In Buenos Aires the *barras bravas* sometimes stand facing their own block to command the singing; in Rome the megaphone man rides the rail and misses every goal; in Poland and the United Kingdom "meetings" are arranged far from the turnstiles while the match unfolds elsewhere. The paradox is almost comical: a furious fidelity to football enacted by people who, in the decisive moments, look away from football.

This is why the nostalgia for "proper" mob football is so stubborn. The talk of bringing back "the good old days", before seating, before family sections, before "womanized" stadia, selects a past as costume.[8] It curates a repertoire of gestures (the march, the chant, the square-go) and insists that these are the real game. The claim to authenticity is theatrical through and through: a carefully handled prop box of masculine signs that must be repeated to count. The repetition is not accidental; it is instrumental. It turns the stand into a workshop where affect is manufactured and where the match is reduced to ambience, a soundtrack to the group's own rule-bound drama: the laws of harassment, of voice, of posture.

Hannah Arendt's report from the Eichmann trial, captured in her 1963 book *Eichmann in Jerusalem*, is a cold lens for this. Arendt (1906–1975) was a German-Jewish political theorist best known for her analyses of totalitarianism, judgment, and responsibility. Reporting for *The New Yorker* on the 1961 Jerusalem trial of Adolf Eichmann (1906–1962), a former SS general who coordinated the deportation logistics of the Nazi "Final Solution", Arendt expected to confront a monstrous architect of evil. Instead, she encountered a drably ordinary defendant, a bureaucrat who presented himself as merely "doing his job". The point here is not to compare the scale, intent, or moral gravity of hooligan violence with the crimes prosecuted in Jerusalem. Rather, it is to use Arendt's diagnosis of the "banality of evil" to show how violence can be sedated by routine and obedience.

Eichmann, she argues, was no Devil. He was a joiner, an administrator of procedures whose great crime was a catastrophic "thoughtlessness", the surrender of judgment to the comfort of rules. Dark play often borrows the same moral anesthetic. It replaces thinking with doing-things-correctly: bring the sticks, never sing the rival's song, never break the agreed numbers, never talk to police, hold the corner. The micro-bureaucracy of away days—buses booked, cash collected, heads counted, stash hidden, signals agreed—creates a hum of ordinary tasks in which extraordinary harm can be folded. No one "chooses" violence in the moment; one fulfils a role. The capo keeps time; the scout spots stragglers; the front line moves on cue. This is, as we saw earlier, the "little war" of the Russian hooligans. In Arendt's sense, the ethical danger is not the eruption of demonic intent but the drowsiness of moral attention by the theatre of procedure. The costume helps: scarves cover faces, identical jackets erase distinction. It becomes easier to do what the role demands when you are, as Eichmann styled himself, merely the functionary of a script.

Does this mean that football harbors an evil nucleus, a ready-to-violence seed that precedes spectacle and culture? Huizinga already tied play to contest and to sacred seriousness. Folk football in medieval streets was combat barely bounded by custom. What the modern laws of the game did, one could argue, was not to abolish the fight but to domesticate it, pressurize it into tactics, timing, and technique. The energy remains convertible. A hard tackle is a handshake with risk, and a derby is spatialized antagonism with civic memory. In that sense, football carries a domestic acknowledgment of the battle: ritual hostility rendered usable. When the frames hold, that energy becomes form—pressing, duels, noise-then-silence. When the frames fail, the same energy runs to cheap transcendence: the thrill of hurting and not being hurt. Remember our pygmy monkeys at the beginning of the chapter.

Roger Caillois helps us see why dark play so often feels like a complete package, a closed circuit of seductions.[9] As we already described in Chapter 1, there is *agon*, the pure contest, rerouted from the grass pitch to the hooligan firm, the table of who stood, who ran, and who owned the street. There is *alea*, the roll of contingency that electrifies away days: will we catch them at the station, will the cordon break, will our lads be lucky? There is *mimicry*, the mask and the part: Stone Island as livery, scarves as insignia, the capo as conductor, the clerk who, like Arendt's Eichmann, disappears into the function he performs. And, finally, there is *ilinx*, vertigo and wooziness, the drum in the ribs, the chemical rush by stimulant regimens, cocaine, amphetamine with beer to facilitate "fronting up", the blur of limbs and smoke when the line collapses and the world tilts. Dark play is compelling because it compresses all four modes into one dense experience and offers it as a shortcut to meaning: contest without craft, chance without consequence, theatre without reflection, dizziness without art. St. Pauli with a shotgun.

•••

We don't want this chapter to be a pious wish to drain the game of danger. It is, instead, a wager about staging. If dark play is not an alien force but a sibling within play, then the only credible response is dramaturgical: to thicken the frames that keep attention on the pitch and to redirect each of Caillois' temptations back into football's own aesthetics. Let agon live where it belongs, in duels, in pressing traps, in the ordered cruelty of a counterattack. Let alea remain the game's sublime uncertainty: the deflection, the post, the stoppage-time ricochet. Let mimicry be carnival, choreography, satire, not militia. Let ilinx be the surge when the net moves and the stand falls forward toward the goal, not toward a stranger's face.

In other words: the fight stays, but its home is the game, or the friendly surrounds of St. Pauli. The laws do not kill play; they keep it from becoming administration for harm. And they ask, of everyone on the stage—players, stewards, capos, writers, you and me—to turn our faces toward the football.

NOTES

1 Carles Vinas and Natxo Parra: *St. Pauli: Another Football is Possible.* Pluto Press, 2020.
2 Even here, the terraces are no utopia. FC St. Pauli's alternative ethos has coexisted with episodes of disorder—pyrotechnics, confrontations, and stadium sanctions—reminding us that the scenes of "inclusive" appropriation we will uncover in this chapter can still edge toward intimidation. The difficulty lies in timing: at what moment do exuberant, nonviolent experiments harden into coercive displays? Freeze the tipping point too early and play calcifies into sanitized conformism; freeze it too late and passion curdles into menace. The task, everywhere in this chapter, is dramaturgical. It is to keep the frame elastic enough for dissent and carnival, but firm enough to refuse harassment and harm.
3 Eric Dunning: *The Roots of Football Hooliganism.* RLE Sports Studies, 1988.
4 Ramón Spaaij: *Understanding Football Hooliganism.* AUP, 2006, and Michel Maffesoli, *The Time of the Tribes.* Sage Publications, 1996.
5 Phil Thornton: *Casuals: Football, Fighting & Fashion: The Story of a Terrace Cult.* Milo Books, 2003.
6 The "demonization" of football culture and the rise of "cool" hooligan (casual) British movies are explored in Emma Poulton: " 'Fantasy Football Hooliganism' in Popular Media". *Media, Culture & Society*, 29/1, 2007, pp. 331–349.
7 Reprinted in Gregory Bateson: *Steps to an Ecology of Mind.* University of Chicago Press, 2000.
8 Anthony King: *The End of the Terraces: The Transformation of English Football.* Leicester University Press, 2001.
9 Roger Caillois: *Man, Play and Games.* University of Illinois Press, 1961.

CHAPTER 9

Platforms

In Europe, football stadiums serve as urban landmarks and pilgrimage sites for fans and tourists eager to see the tangible presence of a club within the city's fabric. Bayern München and Tottenham Hotspur take pride in their modern engineering and design marvels, offering exceptional pitches with meticulously maintained grass. These venues cater not only to players but also to spectators on match days. Modern stadiums ensure easy access and transportation for visitors via private cars or public transit. Historic stadiums like Wembley in London and San Siro in Milano radiate magic, while Estadio Da Luz showcases Portugal's beauty through its seamless integration with the surrounding landscape. During the 2023 and 2024 seasons, Barcelona's iconic Camp Nou was demolished to build a new stadium, leaving the construction site as an open wound in the city's landscape.

Few stadiums in the world possess the lore and mystique of Real Madrid's stadium. Named after Santiago Bernabéu, the club president who shaped the modern myth of the club, the stadium now sits in the heart of Madrid, occupying a prime piece of the city's most expensive real estate, and serving as a must-see destination for tourists and visitors from around the world. El Bernabéu is a historic, venerable stadium, the birthplace of the myth

DOI: 10.1201/9781003636762-10

surrounding one of the greatest clubs in the world, where the Champions League has often seen incredible feats.

Entering the 21st century, El Bernabéu was showing its age. Real Madrid's crown jewel was a somewhat unattractive, functional, and slightly deteriorating structure in an era of modern stadiums designed as gathering places before and after matches. The magic was not gone because the magic is the people and the players all at once, but the venue was no longer a reference point for stadiums worldwide. Real Madrid's then-president, Florentino Pérez, decided to leverage his business skills in engineering and construction to remodel El Bernabéu and turn it into a stadium that would compete with the best in the world. The plan was even more ambitious and significant than merely building a new football stadium. Real Madrid would not just rebuild its stadium; it would transform it into a modern platform to experience the content produced or hosted by the club.

In this chapter, we aim to apply game studies' understanding of the platform concept to analyzing top-tier professional football in Europe from economic and media perspectives. Our knowledge about platforms from game studies draws from research on software environments like Steam or the Apple App Store, as well as game environments like *Fortnite.*[1] Our argument is relatively simple: at the highest level of world football, clubs are no longer just sports clubs but platforms that support the production, distribution, and consumption of various forms of content, all related to, but not exclusive of, the game played by the first team. Modern football is an immensely profitable and enormously expensive sport. Statistically speaking, the only guaranteed route to success is having the best players in the world on the team roster, which requires exorbitant salary wages. Unlike North American professional sports, salaries and leagues are not regulated; therefore, top-tier clubs like Real Madrid can offer wages that exceed those of any other team in their leagues or across Europe.

To sustain their expanding expenses and profit from the insatiable economy of attention and the demand for constant football coverage across all media, modern clubs have begun exploring the corporate world—especially the media and entertainment sectors—for new funding methods. A modern top-tier football club in Europe is no longer just a local symbol of a neighborhood or city. Instead, it functions as a platform for creating and consuming content. It exists within media, whether it owns the content or sources it externally for substantial costs. It promotes its corporate image—from the badge to the kit to the mascot—and uses this for branding across a wide array of products. A modern club leverages the popularity of its key players to generate additional revenue streams. Its stadium serves as the center for these products, a destination that commands increasingly high prices, offering not just a game but an immersive branded experience. Modern football clubs are transforming into entities similar to The Disney Company: a conglomerate of content built around a strong brand with deep emotional ties to a community, drawing in fans and tourists who flock to engage with the brand's offerings. Unlike The Disney Company, football teams have only one brand—the club—making their operational model akin to that of video game platforms. This is the perspective from game studies that we explore in this chapter.

Before we begin, we need to clarify our position. We are not political economists, so some points in this chapter might be better explained by referencing other work in that field, especially regarding branding. We also recognize that our interpretation of the club as a platform is not a direct translation of the concept from game studies. El Bernabéu is not the App Store. However, viewing football clubs as platforms that thrive on the distribution and consumption of various media surrounding the game is a useful perspective. It allows us to place football within the context of current shifts in the video game market, including how games are made, bought, promoted, and circulated. We aim to use the concept of a platform to link what football clubs are doing to the landscape of video games, with the goal of embedding this sport within the same economic and technological environment as other games in the Information Age.

PLATFORMS AND VIDEOGAMES: ECONOMY AND CULTURE

What is a video game platform? In this chapter, we explore the concept of platform through two different modalities. One modality is the software platform, exemplified by Steam as a flagship example of app stores.[2] The other is the experience platform, illustrated by *Fortnite*. Additionally, there are concepts of platforms in game studies, particularly those examining the close connection between historical material technologies, such as the Atari and the Commodore 64, the games produced for those systems, and the culture that emerged from those platforms.[3] Our understanding of platforms in this chapter focuses less on media archaeology and more on the economics of entertainment—or, more accurately, the political economy of play-based entertainment.[4] The concept of a platform is derived from the study of political economy concerning digital technologies and their impact on society since the onset of social media. Researchers like Nieborg and Joseph have articulated the notion of platforms as a means of comprehending the technological advancements behind companies like Facebook and the social, political, and economic effects of these platforms.[5]

A platform is an integrated digital service provider that offers various systems for users to interact with. These systems are interconnected and mutually compatible within the platform but are closed to connections with other systems. The corporations that create platforms monetize this vertical integration through advertising revenue, service subscriptions, and percentages taken from any economic activity within the platform.

For example, the US corporation Meta offers a social media platform with various interoperable services yet incompatible with other social media systems. At the time of writing, Meta owns Facebook, its original social network; Instagram, an image-sharing application; Threads, a microblogging platform; Messenger, an instant messaging app; and WhatsApp, a privacy-focused messaging app.[6] These apps are closely linked and provide every service a social media user might need. They are all free, funded by ad revenue from data mining and tracking user behavior. Facebook, also a platform—although smaller in scope—features a marketplace where users can trade products, allowing Meta to earn revenue by charging fees to sellers.

While these social media platforms may be the most well-known and have produced some of the most socially and politically harmful results of the Silicon Valley revolution in the mid-2000s, videogame platforms differ slightly in scope and align more closely with the phenomenon we argue is emerging in football. There are two types of videogame platforms. The first is the distribution and commercialization platform, such as the App Store or Steam. The second is the experiential platform, with *Fortnite* as the key example, while *Roblox* and *Minecraft* dominate in different spaces.

Steam and the App Store define distribution platforms.[7] These digital services provide means for forcommercializingf digital products through a large install base. Steam has an unparalleled dominance in the distribution of games for the PC market. At the same time, the App Store and Google's Play Store are installed by default on almost all smartphones and tablets and serve as the sole method for installing verified applications on these devices. These distribution platforms offer a range of economic services for the creators of these applications. They track sales metrics over time, display promotions, manage sales, offers, and discounts, and store the software for distribution on their servers. For all these services, distribution platforms charge 30% of the price of the sold software. These platforms earn money from each sale made through their services; revenue developers must budget for this when creating their games, making these distribution platforms enormously profitable.[8]

Distribution platforms are leveraging the importance and convenience of digital distribution to profit from the saturated market of apps and games. Since these platforms only provide support for storing and distributing products, distribution has become easier. At the same time, advances in technology like game engines and software SDKs have made production simpler, leading to an exponential growth in the number of apps and games being distributed through these systems. Consequently, distribution platforms have turned into competitive arenas for visibility. Although they offer some basic curation, the widespread access to all these games and apps floods the market, making it nearly impossible for developers without a strong track record, a large marketing budget, or extraordinary luck to reach their potential audiences.

Experiential platforms operate differently. They do not distribute other games or ludic experiences. These are software products culturally coded as "games". *Fortnite* is the most dominant of these platforms, especially given its outreach to other product domains.[9] Originally, *Fortnite* was a video game that combined third-person shooter multiplayer mechanics with the building and crafting mechanics of games like *Minecraft*. However, the "game" succeeded to such an extent that the software became the home for more activities than just playing the game modes. Structured around seasons, like a TV series, *Fortnite* started offering new content regularly, increasing its revenue through battle passes and microtransactions that allowed users to acquire unique items in games or gain access to some of the new content of the season. The game was originally distributed for free, with a free-to-play economy based on continually refreshed content structured around cinematic changes to the game universe. *Fortnite* thrived during the COVID-19 pandemic, emerging as a cultural and economic powerhouse.[10] Its player base surged significantly during the global lockdowns, transforming it into a social space for many gamers. This third space gained popularity mainly because streamers and content creators used *Fortnite* to produce videos that later were viewed and mimicked by other players.[11] *Fortnite* fostered triple engagement through gameplay, content consumption, and social interaction. Soon, brands like Nike and LEGO partnered with *Fortnite's* developers, Epic Games, to create new content for distribution and commercialization on the platform. Players could enjoy exclusive LEGO-themed games and even wear trendy sneakers as part of their avatars' looks. However, *Fortnite* fostered other interesting partnerships with media creators. The game started launching crossovers with Marvel, allowing players to embody some of the heroes from the movies the studio was releasing rapidly. Musicians also showed interest in the platform, with rap superstar Travis Scott performing a live concert in the game world, attended by up to 50,000 players. *Fortnite* became a space not just for gaming but also for engaging with other media brands and taking part in social events like concerts.

For this chapter, we examine *Fortnite's* platform model to understand football clubs' cultural and economic position in modern gaming. To that end, we propose the following definition: an experiential platform originates from and is fundamentally tied to a game or game-like interactive experience. This game is a foundation for additional content unrelated to its gameplay mechanics. This extra content utilizes the game and the technical framework that supports it (interfaces, chats, online services) to present itself to players. This presentation is commercial, aiming to promote the content without directly monetizing it through the platform. The platform provides visibility and access to this additional content while generating revenue from content providers through sponsorship deals and other revenue streams. Additionally, the platform creates various revenue streams through access fees and other forms of microtransactions.

For example, *Fortnite* is primarily a third-person multiplayer shooter belonging to the battle royale genre. This platform is used by content creators like Marvel and Travis Scott to promote their brand images and products. While these products are not sold directly within the platform, they can be accessed through *Fortnite*. The developers of *Fortnite* earn consistent income from sponsorships related to these services. Additionally, *Fortnite* provides players with various ways to access the game, including battle passes and in-game items that can be purchased in the shop.

Given this definition, modern football clubs in Europe's top tiers can be viewed as platforms. This economic and cultural model greatly influences football clubs' traditional role in European culture.

FOOTBALL CLUBS AS SERVICES

Let's go back to where we began this chapter: the Santiago Bernabéu Stadium in the heart of Madrid.

After the renovation was completed in 2023, the Bernabéu stands as one of the most iconic stadiums in the world. It can seat 78,000 people beneath a retractable roof that allows games to be played regardless of the weather during the harsh Madrid winters. The grass is not only heated but can also be stored underground with a revolutionary greenhouse system that enables the pitch surface to be adapted for various events. The Bernabéu is a football stadium capable of hosting a Taylor Swift concert, a basketball game, American football matches, and tennis tournaments. This versatility could potentially transform the stadium into a fairground and even an emergency hospital.

For visitors to the stadium, whether for a match or just sightseeing, the stadium features a museum, guided tours, a gift shop, and various food options. Additionally, sections of the stadium can be rented for non-spectacle events. From dinners for up to 5000 people on the pitch to exclusive VIP rooms, anyone with enough money can rent a piece of Bernabéu's magic. This magic symbolizes Real Madrid's worldwide brand. Besides the stadium, the club owns a TV platform, manages several successful social media accounts, and has stakes in various print media. Real Madrid has numerous corporate sponsors that use the club's facilities and players to leverage their popularity for promotional purposes.

Real Madrid is more than just a brand.[12] Their newly renovated stadium symbolizes an economic strategy designed to counter the influence of state-sponsored clubs in European football. A state-sponsored club is a football club purchased by a government, typically from the Middle East.[13] Following the template of Manchester City's takeover by Abu Dhabi's sovereign fund, these ownership models infuse historic clubs with capital, enabling them to recruit the world's top players while investing in their academies, women's teams, and building new stadiums. The presence of these deep pockets in European football has disrupted the historical balance of the 20th century, allowing clubs like Manchester City, PSG, or Newcastle to suddenly compete economically with teams that once dominated the income hierarchy in Europe, such as Bayern München, Manchester United, or Real Madrid.[14]

This state money significantly differs from the private ownership schemes of capital firms in the United States, such as Fenway's group ownership of Liverpool or the whims of wealthy individuals from the Russian oligarch era in the Premier League.[15] Capital firms cannot invest endless amounts of money in a team; they always expect a return on investment to satisfy stakeholders. The oligarch money has also dried up, leading to very few clubs owned by wealthy individuals. State-sponsored clubs have access to a state's political and economic power, allowing them to pay wages beyond market logic while bypassing the supposedly strict economic fair play rules set by UEFA and FIFA.

The challenge posed by these state-sponsored clubs shook the old aristocracy of European football. When PSG purchased Neymar from FC Barcelona for a staggering 222 million euros, we witnessed a cultural and economic shift in the game. Historic clubs like Barcelona found themselves economically disadvantaged in attracting and retaining talented players worldwide. The traditional top clubs were now sidelined by the financial power of national investment funds, which acquired historic teams and transformed them into economic powerhouses capable of changing the dynamics of local leagues and European football. Manchester City and PSG, teams with a relatively short history but previously charming local clubs, emerged as challengers to the old European aristocracy, thanks to the deep pockets of Middle Eastern states.

Despite its many successes, Real Madrid is a remnant of a bygone era. As of now, it remains a member-owned club. While the club has always benefited from political decisions made by the Madrid community and the Spanish state, Real Madrid is not a conventional state-owned club. Its economy continues to rely on being a football club, leveraging assets both on and off the pitch, and building a brand and culture that attracts players worldwide. Winning shapes the identity of Real Madrid, notably winning the Champions League. However, that identity is threatened by the rise of state-owned clubs. Beginning in the second decade of the 21st century, Real Madrid experienced challenges to its identity and dominance, necessitating new ideas and economic approaches.

The solution involved delving deeper into Real Madrid's history while giving it a modern twist. To generate revenue that would allow the team to compete with sovereign funds, Real Madrid committed to becoming an experience platform.

No other team in the world has historically understood the concept of a platform quite like Real Madrid. Santiago Bernabéu, the president who transformed the club from a local team into a global household name, recognized the significance of having an identifiable stadium located at the heart of a city that was also the center of political and economic power. Bernabéu also understood the importance of the Champions League earlier than anyone else, viewing it not just as a competition but as a means to craft an image and a legend that would resonate with people even before the rise of global television broadcasting. Real Madrid developed a brand by recognizing the aspirational and emotional nature of football. It leveraged that brand, that legend, to create what we understand as an experiential platform: a collection of monetized services rooted in a core ludic experience, specifically the football team.

With the rise of state-owned clubs, this platform exposed its limitations. The stadium was outdated, and the legend's appeal wasn't always enough to attract talent or sufficient funding to compete with wealthy newcomers. The solution was to overhaul the platform, aligning it more closely with an experiential platform like *Fortnite*.

The club already had several conditions in place for becoming a platform: the core of the experience was the football team, with matches at Bernabéu being a ritual that provided identity and a location for the team. Spectators would gather at the stadium to see the world's best players compete.[16] The new stadium would be more than just a sports venue; it would entertain audiences for hours surrounding the main event, with dining and shopping opportunities, all curated and branded by Real Madrid, contributing to a diversified revenue stream.[17]

However, there is only football twice a week in the Bernabéu at most. Real Madrid has transformed its primary physical asset into a tourism and experiences platform to compete with clubs supported by oil-rich economies. Thanks to the engineering marvels of the new stadium, Real Madrid secured a revenue stream that includes fashion events, other sports like tennis, and music concerts. The two biggest stars during the opening of the new Bernabéu were French striker Kylian Mbappé, who signed with Real in the summer of 2024, and Taylor Swift, who led the most popular concert to date at the Bernabéu.

The economy of top-flight football can no longer be sustained solely by the game played on the field. The enormous salaries earned by star players and the costs associated with maintaining a competitive elite team require funding far beyond the meager traditional streams of player transfers, matchday tickets, and TV rights. Modern elite clubs operate with budgets nearing ten figures, and everything is for sale or can be monetized. Consequently, football clubs have evolved into experiential platforms. A club is no longer just a local football team, playing with a group of kids from nearby neighborhoods. Clubs have transformed into global brands, capable of monetizing all their assets through media production, blockchain tokens, fashion drops, and multimedia collaborations, while also serving as hubs for other brands to reach new audiences. Their squads resemble a mock UN, featuring the best players from around the world, all competing not only for the now somewhat less prestigious national leagues but also for international cups, such as the Champions League and the World Club Cup.

Like all the other juggernauts, Real Madrid has become similar to *Fortnite*. Its stadium now serves as a venue not just for football, but also for media consumption and production that extends well beyond the sport. The aim is for fans to stay within the Real Madrid ecosystem: they watch the team, follow the stars on social media, view the documentaries created by the in-house media company, attend matches, and, while doing so, purchase tokens, whether physical or digital, as a sign of loyalty. Furthermore, their entertainment options are conveniently situated in the same place they watch the game. They can visit Bernabéu to watch tennis or attend a concert—all hosted by Real Madrid, though not sponsored. This goes beyond mere branding; it is a platforming operation. Ideally, the Real Madrid fan spends their leisure time and economic activities around the club, whether attending matches, wearing their merchandise, or going to the stadium for other events.

Stadiums have always served as venues for large-scale concerts and events. Why should we reconsider this perception? We argue that the economic pressures and opportunities of contemporary top-flight football have prompted clubs to intentionally develop their stadiums as platforms for economic growth. This strategy now focuses on viewing the club's physical location as a source of revenue tied to its main brand. The situation regarding the stadium mirrors that of media rights: while clubs sell their image rights to broadcasters through the collective agreements of national leagues, they retain the rights to their players, training sessions, sponsorship videos, and similar venues. This enables clubs to create content and monetize it via social media, YouTube, or their own TV broadcasting channels. This multimedia initiative is not merely a branding effort; it serves as a method to generate revenue streams that complement ticket sales and broadcasting rights while also aligning the leisure consumption of their fans with the club.

An interesting, although anecdotal, example is the alliances between clubs and crypto tech companies during the early 2020s.[18] Clubs sought to capitalize on the popularity of NFTs and other similar digital assets by creating collections of images for which they held the rights and selling them to their fans. The presence of crypto funding and products has thankfully diminished after the collapse of that crypto wave, but the idea persists: football clubs are interested in microtransactions within the media ecosystem in which they operate, aiming to create novel revenue streams that enable them to lock their fans into their own brand/platform and continue growing economically, which is essential to attracting the talent that can win championships.

The attention elite football clubs pay to leveraging their brand through various methods of engaging fans in a content distribution strategy transforms them into platforms. Clubs serve as experiential platforms rather than technical ones. This means that while clubs do not always own the actual infrastructure of the platform, they establish strategic alliances with other media producers to utilize the platform for content distribution. These alliances connect football clubs with subsidiary companies that assist in producing the distributed content. Ultimately, this makes football clubs slightly different from video game platforms. *Fortnite*, *Roblox*, and *Minecraft* are all platforms that vertically integrate technical infrastructure with experiential content. Epic Games owns the Unreal Engine that powers *Fortnite*, granting them complete control over content distribution. Football clubs do not yet possess that level of vertical control. At the same time, recent stadium developments by top-flight clubs in Europe demonstrate that clubs recognize that owning a brand and a physical platform enables them to create competitive revenue streams.

Once again, Real Madrid leads the pack in this regard: although they have sold the rights to monetize aspects of the Bernabéu, they still own the stadium. They also maintain a strong grip on their players' image rights, which has been standard in their contracts since the era of the Galácticos (Beckham, Figo, Zidane, Ronaldo) in the 2000s. The club sells merchandise and receives a generous share from the kit manufacturer, but they also retain the rights to use their image on other apparel that is not produced by their main sponsor. Furthermore, they own their media house, which creates content for a TV channel. Real Madrid is not Epic Games … yet. However, it illustrates how platformization is shaping the way modern football economies at the highest level are reorienting themselves.

The ideal scenario for these clubs is to create the sporting equivalent of *Fortnite*: a physical and cultural space where people continually spend money and time engaging with the main brand (*Fortnite*/the Club), while also consuming products from relevant sponsors and expanding their engagement to other forms of leisure. Ideally, free time is spent on this platform, which directly or indirectly attracts revenue to the club. The club then transforms into more than just a local sports association or the emblem of a city, country, or nation. It evolves into an experiential platform that aspires to achieve total engagement from people.

In other parts of this book, we discuss the close relationship between football and identity, so we will not cover the implications of the shift from clubs to platforms from that perspective here. Instead, we want to examine how the platformization of football clubs can yield short-term benefits for football, particularly for elite clubs. However, that success may pose risks to the culture and economics of the game.

As I write these words, the video game industry is facing one of its periodic crises. Up to 40,000 individuals have been let go from their jobs between January 1st and May 1, 2025, and the industry's revenue has dropped to pre-COVID-19 levels. This crisis is complex, and we will not explore all of its causes here. However, one significant aspect to highlight is the disruption that platforms inflict on media ecosystems in entertainment. There are two key data points to consider in grasping this crisis in the video game industry: first, video game developers struggle to balance their budgets due to the cuts that platforms take for distributing products, in addition to the marketing costs necessary to gain visibility within these distribution systems. Second, players tend to shy away from new experiences and stick to platforms that offer both entertainment and social value. In other words, players prefer to remain in *Fortnite* rather than try out new games.

How can we translate this into the admittedly quite different media and entertainment ecology of football? If we accept the premise that elite football clubs are establishing experiential platforms, we can suggest that this platformization will lead to, or is already creating, a significant schism in football. Elite clubs will effectively transform into platforms due to their economic resources and global audiences. Real Madrid, FC Barcelona, Manchester United, and Paris Saint Germain are already global platforms, and many other elite teams are on similar trajectories.[19] This situation leaves other clubs resembling non-platform games. They have an audience, a following, and a cultural presence, but their reach is limited by the harsh economy of the game. Without platform-derived income, these clubs cannot compete to attract or retain world-class talent, which will gravitate toward platform clubs, thus limiting the potential for these non-platform clubs to compete or evolve into platforms themselves.

We are moving toward a football culture where elite clubs act as platforms that not only compete but also collaborate exclusively with other platforms, while the remaining clubs struggle to survive on the scraps of the attention economy left behind by these giants. The all-encompassing experiences created by these platforms overshadow smaller experiences, especially smaller clubs, ultimately leading to an ecosystem dominated by just a few profitable platforms competing against each other, punctuated by the occasional charming success story of an outsider. The attempts by some clubs to establish a European Superleague that mimics the closed-league structure of US sports, excluding clubs too small to become platforms, exemplify the effects of platformization.

More dangerously, platforms tend to fracture ecosystems. The video game industry in the mid-2020s shows how players prefer to stick with familiar games rather than trying new ones. Similarly, there's a risk that football fans will be limited to narrower platform experiences. Why would a global audience be interested in supporting or following RC Celta (Spain), Randers (Denmark), or even historic teams like Napoli or Fiorentina (both Italian)? Major platform clubs offer everything a worldwide crowd wants, neatly packaged and delivered as a single message. Fans don't even need to watch the actual games: it's enough to view highlights, follow social media, and buy merchandise to feel connected to the platform. Just as *Fortnite* has engaged generations of players in an immersive environment, Real Madrid aims to lock fans into a single identity that excludes other clubs, forms of fandom, and even different experiences.

This doomsday scenario is frequently criticized in modern football. The overemphasis on the Champions League compared to national leagues, along with the global tours that top clubs do during preseason to promote their brand internationally, all point to the game being reduced to platforms that serve the audience's desires without requiring them to look elsewhere.

Let us conclude this chapter with a more personal reflection. During the 2024–2025 season, I (Miguel) was lucky to hold a season ticket for FC Barcelona, one of the clubs I have been writing about. While the experience was amazing because of my traditional, family-oriented, and political loyalty to the club, it was also eye-opening. Before each match, FC Barcelona plays the club anthem, a highly political song that links the club with Catalan identity. The lyrics say that the "blaugrana people", *la gent blaugrana*, are part of a brotherhood united by a flag, regardless of their backgrounds. The original meaning of this song was very political: it represents a nation trying to bring its people together, no matter where they come from, under several cultural symbols. FC Barcelona's anthem is a key part of the Catalan nation-building identity.[20]

Or it was. Every match day, surrounded by crowds of tourists from around the world, I realized that these masses of fans who did not understand the lyrics of the song are the new *gent blaugrana*, united not by the ethos of the "more than a club" spirit, but by the economics of an experiential platform. Attending a match became another token to consume in their ongoing engagement with the offerings of this platform. As a long-time supporter, a Romantic one at that, I felt the unavoidable ambiguity of contemporary football: for clubs to create the emotional experiences I enjoyed during that season, part of the club's identity was transformed into a platform. This platform financed the club and the emotions. We know what the benefits are. But what is the cost?

NOTES

1 Srnicek, 2017.
2 Joseph, 2021; Joseph et al., 2023.
3 Montfort and Bogost, 2009.
4 Nieborg and Poell, 2018.
5 Nieborg, 2015, 2021.
6 Nieborg and Helmond, 2019.
7 D. J. Joseph, 2018.
8 Thorhauge, 2023a, 2023b.
9 Sidorenko-Bautista et al., 2025; White, 2024.
10 Soto de la Cruz et al., 2008.
11 Ducheneaut et al., 2007; Steinkuehler and Williams, 2006.
12 Baena, 2018, 2023; Mañas-Viniegra, 2018.

13 Krzyzaniak, 2018.
14 Mirkovic et al., 2025.
15 Rohde and Breuer, 2017.
16 Baena, 2023.
17 Bernabéu's remodeling was not a painless success story. At the moment of writing this note, in November 2025, Real Madrid is still battling local neighbors over noise pollution. The club had to abandon plans to build a large underground parking lot due to legal obstacles.
18 Chen, 2025.
19 The Deloitte Football Money League (www.deloitte.com/uk/en/services/consulting-financial/analysis/deloitte-football-money-league.html) provides a critical insight on the economics of the superclub. The Swiss Ramble newsletter (https://swissramble.substack.com) provides the best accessible financial analysis of football.
20 Hamil et al., 2010.

Coda

LEAVING THE PITCH

We have both left too many stadiums with our throats sandpapered and our notebooks smudged, walking into cold nights that felt longer than they were. On some of those walks home, we were the kind of fans who drift silently through the city, trying not to scare away a fragile happiness. On others, we were the kind who argue with lampposts. We are scholars who love football and fans who can't quite stop turning the screws on the question: why does this game move us, and how is it made to move us? It's a stubborn double life. The game pulls you in until you're living week-to-week on lineups and form and that impossible pass you replay on your phone. Meanwhile, the scholar in you wants to pry the game open, to see its gears and its levers, to name the patterns that the game keeps teasing you with.

This is not an even split. The fan wins most weekends. The scholar comes back on Mondays, with highlighters. Our partners and kids live with both of us. They've learned the shape of our calendar, the way dinner shifts from Saturday to Sunday depending on the fixtures, the way we trail off mid-sentence when a center-back checks their shoulder and the press angle

DOI: 10.1201/9781003636762-11

suddenly matters more than whatever we were saying. Loving football like this is a constant struggle and a joy, and it bleeds into the rest of life. It is not only the spectacle; it's the desire to unlock its innermost secrets, the feeling that if we just look closely enough at one more sequence, we might finally understand how intelligence looks when it runs.

If the book you've just read has a heartbeat, it is the tension we live with every day: between rules and freedom, between mission and wandering, between ordered play and wild play. We write code in our heads for how football works; then someone—Pedri, Marta, Messi, Rapinoe—breaks it with a first touch. We praise the choreographer in the dugout and then fall to our knees for the soloist who invents a different ending. We want to win, obviously. But the journey there and back again is its own circular heaven and nightmare: hope, dread, patience, fury, and a peculiar, stubborn belief that next time the same shapes will yield a different answer.

Sometimes it feels religious. The long walk out of Egypt—bad away days, injuries, those January matches that test what you think love means—toward a promised land that might be a trophy with big ears or the signing of the next superstar. You pick your enemies with care; you call that care tradition. And always there is the social battle around the game: money, power, labor, the city, who gets in and who gets priced out, who carries the banners and who signs the deals.

Sometimes the metaphor isn't just a metaphor. There are mountains in this game. Sinai-mountains. Places where you are called, but who charged them there? The demand for faith itself, the command to keep going when the sand bites. We think of Moses pleading to see the glory and being granted, not the face, but the passing shadow. We think of a club wandering its own desert: Real Madrid's 40-year feeling through the wilderness to the borders of Canaan compressed into 12 seasons, the pilgrimage toward *La Décima*, May 24, 2014. This was their tenth Champions League crown, oh boy. Every spring a new Sinai, every elimination another circle of grime around the camp. And then Lisbon, minute 92:48, the corner from Luca Modrić like a prayer on a thread, and Sergio Ramos rising as if he had been told, on some mountain, to keep climbing. That header wasn't a goal; it was an answer to a plea. The promised land had goalposts, and it was mesmerizing.

There's also an old, unsolved problem that sits in our work: intimacy and distance. You love something so much you want more of it, and then you learn to step back to write about it. You make it different in order to grasp the sameness that has been your companion. Dissection is not betrayal, but it reshapes attachment. The risk is turning joy into homework. The reward is learning to see more joy.

•••

We have both stood in living rooms with a baby on a hip, shushing a match, and we have both delivered lectures the morning after a midweek fixture on two hours of sleep. We have learned to take notes that look like set-piece diagrams and grocery lists at once. And we have learned, sometimes awkwardly, that the rhythms of family life and the rhythms of the game are not natural allies. What helps is honesty. Football is unreasonable, and love survives unreasonable things best when it isn't pretending to be reasonable.

The game itself lives inside an unreasonable tension. The rules promise order, the game guarantees surprise. Coaches draw arrows while players go looking for shortcuts. Models predict; ankles wobble; wind changes; someone sees a corridor that wasn't there seconds ago. That tension between constraint and invention isn't an inconvenience to be ironed out. It's the source of the game's charge. And living with football as a fan-scholar is practicing the same tension in miniature. We oscillate between system and story, spreadsheet and song. We keep learning how to hold both.

Games are laboratories for intelligence. Football is not a board game and it's not a perfect benchmark for AI. But "Move 37" in Go gave us a way to talk about the future arriving sideways: a move that was statistically sound but, more importantly, beautiful because it broke our sense of sense. We asked: what is football's Move 37? And we offered one candidate in a small moment—Pedri's first-touch pass against Switzerland that looked not at where anyone stood but at where their momentum would soon forbid them to be. That pass didn't feel like a calculation. It felt like a glimpse of time.

We are closer than ever to machines that can help us understand the game, if not play it like Marta or Zlatan. The data revolution gave us new lenses: expected goals as a way to price a chance; space-occupancy models that tell us which pockets breathe; tracking data that reveals press triggers and passing lanes that television hides. When Thomas Tuchel taught a Chelsea side to shoot less and score more, it wasn't magic. It was a model of chance quality translated into training and selection. When Germany led their World Cup group in xG and still went home, it wasn't proof that data is blind. It was the spine of the sport asserting itself: low scoring, high variance, the stubborn fact that good chances still need finishing and that finishing is hard.

We believe in these lenses. We also believe in caution. All models are wrong; some are useful, and some are flattening. Data is a way of seeing, and every way of seeing makes something else less visible. If football's intelligence is entangled—embodied, spatial, emotional—then the trick is to use new measurements to illuminate rather than replace what the game already knows. Let xG be a flashlight, not a map.

Once you start thinking like a game designer, you can't unsee the metagame. It's not just how teams play within the rules; it's how they play with the rules, and how everything around the match—media, politics, stadium design—shapes what happens in it. We tried to show that metagaming isn't a sideshow; it's the game's nervous system.

Consider the oldest trick in the book: wasting time. The USWNT, a team whose identity was all forward motion, learned to take the ball to the corner and refuse the game at the end of a match. It is perfectly legal and deeply irritating because it narrows the possibility space to a single, tedious loop. But that, too, is football. Or consider a different kind of metagame: Hansi Flick's Barcelona riding a very high defensive line in the season when semi-automatic VAR tightened offside calls to the centimeter. That was playing with the medium, trusting that technology's cold eye would punish any runner's single mistimed step. It was beautiful in its own ruthless way and a reminder that technology is just another field condition to be learned and bent.

Metagaming runs beyond the laws and the cameras. It lives in press conferences that plant ideas in referees' heads, in contract clauses that manage image rights, in every decision a club makes about how to tour a continent or launch a jersey. You don't have to like all of it. But if you love the sport, it helps to know that the game is bigger than 90 minutes—and that some of the most decisive moves are made before the whistle blows.

Dark play is the evil twin that cast a cloud over life-expanding playfulness. Our creed is symbolic violence, the ritual combat inside the white lines: friends and co-workers Monday through Friday and yet fierce enemies for 90 minutes plus Ramos Time. Different tactics and different esoteric readings of the same scripture of one God: "the ball is round". Battle it out, shake hands, go home. We dismiss the false believers in dark play because they turn from football proper toward banal violence: racism, homophobia, hooliganism, pitch invasions that harm, the cheap thrill of breaking a face instead of breaking a press. That is not play; that is the refusal of play.

If there was a hill we chose in this book, it was Law 11. Offside is both a riddle and a metronome; it keeps the rhythm, and it complicates it. It pulls individuals and collectives into the same problem: can you time your run to the heartbeat of a moving line? Can you move the line with a gesture? Filippo Inzaghi lived right there, at the edge of permission. Franco Baresi lived there too, walking the line like a tightrope with a back four attached to his belt. The pitch expands and contracts around that tightrope; the game becomes a duel between a single heartbeat and a synchronized pulse.

The offside rule is beautiful because it produces meaningful agency for everyone: the runner, the line, the assistant's flag, the referee's reading of intention. VAR complicated this. It traded some human fallibility for objectivity. Sometimes it robbed us of the right kind of uncertainty and gave us the wrong kind: the dead air between a goal and a confirmation. Sometimes, as with Barcelona's high line, it opened a tactical frontier. Our position, as fans and scholars, is a little boring and very human: keep the interpretive space alive. Let technology assist without swallowing judgment. A game whose beauty depends in part on fallible interpretation shouldn't outsource too much of its soul.

•••

We stand in the shadow of the Estadio Bernabéu in Madrid, old and new. The renovation is a marvel: a roof that opens, a pitch that hibernates underground, a stadium that can become an arena for almost anything. It is also a signpost. Modern clubs are no longer only clubs. They are experiential platforms, hubs where media, merchandise, travel, sponsorship, concerts, and sport interlock. Fortnite with a cathedral and a better set-piece routine.

We're not naïve. Elite football costs what it costs, and the era of state-backed clubs changed the economics of success. Real Madrid's answer—turn the stadium into a 24/7 platform—was rational and in many ways brilliant. It is also a risk to the ecosystem. Platforms tend to hoard attention. When a few giants can offer everything, the middle thins out. Why learn the taste of RC Celta when you can sip a global brand that pours all year?

We've felt this up close. One of us held a season ticket in Barcelona while the club played away from Camp Nou. The anthem still spoke of a brotherhood united by a flag regardless of origin; the stands were, more than ever, a parade of tourists, phones aloft, consuming a bucket-list moment. Nothing about that is evil. Much of it pays for the kids' academy and the women's team. But you can feel the shift from citizens to users, from club to platform. The work ahead of us—fans, scholars, clubs—is to hold on to local meaning while we cash global checks. Support the small and the stubborn. Keep football as a public language, not only a premium product.

And then there's the possibility space. It is a designer's way to name what players live: the set of actions that feel available right now. The formal space (what the rules allow) is huge; the perceived space (what a player actually sees) is smaller and constantly shifting. The art of coaching is shaping the perceived space—teaching players to see what they don't yet see, rehearsing patterns that open doors at full speed, building a shared map that can bend under pressure without breaking.

This is why kids start 3v3 on a small pitch with small goals. Fewer bodies, slower storms. The game's grammar can be learned without getting drowned by its literature. It's why rondos work: a simple, cruel exercise that teaches you to see two passes ahead and to anticipate where pressure will come from. It's why a Footbonaut makes sense for ten minutes and never for an hour: you isolate a decision to sharpen the edge and then you go back to the storm, where the choices are real.

•••

We are happy that Miguel made it out alive from playing the Game of Switches. He sacrificed for the sake of scholarship, and what we learned from that little monster of a design is that an emergent web of branching paths—endless, glittering, full of potential wrong turns—can suddenly flip into a single linear road by way of smart tactics, a shimmer of luck, and a pinch of magic. That's football, too: multiverse, then tunnel; chaos, then one run, one pass, one finish.

And part of that magic has a name: Mario Zagallo. Before the midfield was a department, it was a revelation. Brazil's modernism bending a 4-2-4 into a 4-3-3, and Zagallo's footwork and positioning doing the quiet carpentry between the lines. Passing, blocking, and the geometry of presence. To "move the air", as Cruyff lamented and admired, is to make space breathe where it didn't. The midfield makes you read the play like a book, exploit it like a game, and rewatch it like a thrilling action movie. Once you see that hinge between defense and attack, you cannot unsee it; the whole match becomes a novel with better chase scenes.

Coaches, at their best, are cartographers of possibility. Pep Guardiola divides the pitch into 20 zones and fills them with rules-of-thumb that become instincts. He doesn't decide the story; he sets the stage where a certain kind of story is likely. Jürgen Klopp does the same with rest-defense and pressing triggers. Mourinho and Simeone carve different maps that shrink the enemy's possibilities until a counter looks like fate. Great coaches see new maps first.

There are players who redraw the map mid-sprint. The ones who find diagonal lanes that didn't exist, who turn their hips and history at once, who treat the ball like a question nobody else heard. Those are the ones we travel for and write about. Data will keep trying to follow them. It is allowed to be late.

It would be easy to spend an outro talking only about passes and platforms. But the game's future is also made in labor disputes, in boardrooms, in city councils, in the quiet work of youth coaches who keep kids in love with a team sport in an era of infinite screens. It lives in the growth of the women's game and the overdue fights over pay, resources, scheduling, and respect that have changed football more than any tactical trend in the last decade. It lives in the ethics of sponsorship and state ownership, in the accounting tricks that stretch the meaning of "fair play", in fan groups that organize for governance and against ticket hikes.

Being a fan-scholar means naming the contradictions and picking some sides. We can love elite football without pretending it is a neutral marketplace. We can hold two ideas at once: that elite clubs are doing extraordinary work in high-performance environments, and that the sport owes more to the communities that built it than a victory parade every other year. We can use the vocabulary of games to ask political questions: who controls the rules? Who benefits from a narrower possibility space? Where does the meta close doors instead of opening them?

There is a climate piece here, too. Football's calendar, travel habits, pitch maintenance, and televised footprint all have costs. The promised land can't be a scorched one. Part of the next decade's tactical innovation will be organizational: calendars that breathe, competitions that stop treating players as content, tours that make sense for more than revenue.

Writing about football as work has made us love it better. Not more—better. There are days when analysis steals hours from awe. And then there are days when a term like third-man run or cover shadow snaps into focus in a way that actually amplifies the feeling in your chest. We used to watch only the ball; now we watch the nearest six bodies, the line of the ball and the line of sight. We used to shout at referees; now we also watch their diagonals and the way they keep the game's temperature. This is not a replacement for fandom. It's an addition.

The intimacy-distance problem doesn't go away. You still have to choose when to put the pen down and just sing. You still owe people in your life a day without football now and then. You still need to forgive your club for being a corporation and your rival for being happy sometimes. But learning to see differently has made the game sturdier for us. It has given us a way to sit with defeat that isn't just superstition and to sit with victory that isn't just relief.

•••

It's easy to imagine a football that slides further into platform logic. Semi-automatic offside becomes standard. Augmented reality overlays on broadcast and in-stadium glasses annotate every press trigger. Training grounds hum with computer vision and injury-prediction models; recruiting becomes Moneyball-plus. The matchday app becomes a wallet, a guide, a surveillance device. The Super League returns under a different name, better dressed. The middle tier of clubs becomes farm systems. Fans become users, users become metrics.

It's also easy to imagine a football that metabolizes technology without losing itself. VAR rules narrow to truly "clear and obvious" interventions and are enforced with the humility of fallible tools. Offside stays human at the edges, even with lines. Clubs use data to protect player health rather than only performance. The women's game keeps expanding, reshaping old assumptions about what football is supposed to look like. Grassroots clubs, supporter-owned, municipally supported, and stubbornly local, become the sport's R&D labs for culture. Leagues learn to price tickets like public theaters. Broadcasts get better at teaching people how to watch without turning them into accountants.

Both futures are plausible. The difference will come from choices made by federations, clubs, broadcasters, players' unions—and by us. If we treat ourselves as customers first, we'll be treated that way. If we keep playing in parks and showing up for second-division Tuesdays and choosing fandoms that reflect our politics as well as our appetites, the meta shifts.

Somewhere in all this a "Move 37 of football" may arrive. It might be an algorithmic insight—a pattern no human staff saw that becomes the seed of a new pressing scheme. But we suspect it will look more like a person. It will be an Inzaghi who never looks offside until it's too late, a Baresi who moves a line with a glance, a midfielder who passes like they've got a time machine in their ankle. When it happens, the models will explain something about it. They won't explain it away.

You don't need permission from us, but here it is anyway: learn the vocabulary and use it to love the game harder. Watch the ball and the shadows. Enjoy xG as a way to argue on the walk home. Notice when a team plays the rules and when it plays with them. Cheer for your club and keep a standing appointment with your local team, your kids' team, the women's team two neighborhoods over. Keep your eye on who writes the rules and what those rules make possible.

Teach a kid a rondo. Go to a stadium you haven't been to and eat what they eat there. If your club becomes a platform, take what you need and give when you can, but don't be afraid to say when enough is enough. Remember that a referee having a good game is part of the beauty. Remember that a goal disallowed by a human line can sometimes be as just as one disallowed by a computer's. Remember that fair and beautiful are cousins, not twins.

Above all, keep the game open. That's the through-line in everything we have argued. Openness in rules: enough interpretation to allow invention. Openness in culture: enough space for clubs that aren't brands to be more than feeder systems. Openness in technology: tools that assist rather than dictate. Openness in you, as in time to be a fan without turning yourself into a performance analyst on a Sunday morning.

Football screams for admiration of the rule that turns freedom into art; a habit of seeing spaces where others see only lines; a suspicion of systems that call themselves inevitable; a willingness to be wrong at full voice; a gratitude for the player who makes time behave; a patience for the referee who has to choose in real time; a hope, still, for the long walk that ends in a cup and starts again the next day with a ball off the wall.

Bibliography

Aragão e Pina, J., Passos, A. Araújo, D., & Maynard, M. T. (2018). Football refereeing: An integrative review. *Psychology of Sport and Exercise*, 35, 10–26.

Archetti, E. (2016). *Masculinidades: Fútbol, polo y tango en la Argentina*. CreateSpace Publishing.

Arendt, H. (1963). *Eichmann in Jerusalem*. The Viking Press.

Backe, H.-J. (2012). Narrative rules? Story logic and the structures of games. *Literary and Linguistic Computing*, 27(3), 243–260.

Baena, V. (2016). Online and mobile marketing strategies as drivers of brand love in sports teams. *International Journal of Sports Marketing and Sponsorship*, 17(3), 202–218. https://doi.org/10.1108/IJSMS-08-2016-015

Baena, V. (2018). The importance of CSR practices carried out by sport teams and its influence on brand love: The Real Madrid Foundation. *Social Responsibility Journal*, 14(1), 61–79. https://doi.org/10.1108/SRJ-11-2016-0205

Baena, V. (2023). The importance of social identification through digital marketing to cultivate emotional attachment towards the brand: Evidence from the Real Madrid, F.C. *International Journal of Marketing, Communication and New Media*, 13, 56–76.

Barclay, P. (2015). *The Life and Times of Herbert Chapman: The Story of One of Football's Most Influential Figures*. W&N.

Barnett, V., & Hilditch, S. (1993). The effect of an artificial pitch surface on home team performance in football (soccer). *Journal of the Royal Statistical Society Series A: Statistics in Society*, 156(1), 39–50. https://doi.org/10.2307/2982859

Bateson, G. (1972). *Steps to an Ecology of Mind*. Jason Aronson Inc.

Beavan, A., Fransen, J., Spielmann, J., Mayer, J., Skorski, S., & Meyer, T. (2019). The Footbonaut as a new football-specific skills test: Reproducibility and age-related differences in highly trained youth players. *Science and Medicine in Football*, 3(3), 177–182. https://doi.org/10.1080/24733938.2018.1548772

Best, D. (1988). Sport is not art. In Morgan, W. J. & Meier, K. V. *Philosophic Inquiry in Sport*. Human Kinetics Publishers.

Biermann, C. (2019). *Football Hackers: The Science and Art of a Data Revolution*. Blink Publishing.

Boluk, S. & Le Mieux, P. (2017), *Metagaming: Playing, Competing, Spectating, Cheating, Trading, Making, and Breaking Videogames*. University of Minnesota Press.

Bordner, S. (2015). Call 'Em as they are: What's wrong with blown calls and what to do about them. *Journal of the Philosophy of Sport*, 42(1), 101–120.

Borges, J. L. (1989). *El fútbol a sol y sombra*. In *Obras Completas*. Emecé.

Boyer, S., MacMahon, C., Récopé, M. & Rix-Lièvre, G. (2020). The assistant referees' activity in refereeing elite football: Preoccupations when not judging offside. *Psychology of Sport and Exercise*, 48, 101662.

Brillinger, D. (2007). A potential function approach to the flow of play in soccer. *Journal of Quantitative Analysis in Sports*, 3(1), 1–19.

Caillois, R. (1961). *Man, Play and Games*. University of Illinois Press.

Carter, M., Gibbs, M., & Harrop, M. (2012). Metagames, paragames and orthogames: a new vocabulary. *Proceedings of the International Conference on the Foundations of Digital Games*.

Chen, R., & Davidson, N.P. (2022). English Premier League manager perceptions of video assistant referee (VAR) decisions during the 2019–2020 season. *Soccer and Society*, 23(1), 44–55.

Chen, C. (2025). Contesting fan tokens under crypto-capitalism: How sport NFT furthers the hypercommodification of fandom. *International Journal of Sports Marketing and Sponsorship*, 26(2), 254–272. https://doi.org/10.1108/IJSMS-03-2023-0057

Clark, N. & Anthropy, A. (2014). *A Game Design Vocabulary*. CRC Press.

Collett, M. (2003). *The Complete Record of the FA Cup*. Sportsbooks.

Collins, H. (2010). The philosophy of umpiring and the introduction of decision-aid technology. *Journal of the Philosophy of Sport*, 37(2), 135–146.

Consalvo, M. (2009). There is no magic circle. *Games and Culture*, 4(4), 408–417.

Cox, M. (2019). *Zonal Marking: The Making of Modern European Football*. HarperCollins Publishers Ltd.

Critchley, S. (2017). *What We Think About When We Think About Soccer*. Penguin Books.

Deuze, M., & Prenger, M. (2019). *Making Media: Production, Practices, and Professions*. Amsterdam University Press. https://doi.org/10.5117/9789462988118

Ducheneaut, N., Moore, R. J., & Nickell, E. (2007). Virtual "third places": A case study of sociability in massively multiplayer games. *Computer Supported Cooperative Work (CSCW)*, 16(1), 129–166. https://doi.org/10.1007/s10606-007-9041-8

Dunning, E. (1988). *The Roots of Football Hooliganism*. RLE Sports Studies.

Elcombe, T. L. (2012). Sport, Aesthetic Experience, and Art as the Ideal Embodied Metaphor. *Journal of the Philosophy of Sport*, 39(2), 201–217.

Elias, G. S., Garfield. R., & Gutschera, K. R. (2012). *Characteristics of Games*. The MIT Press.

Ensum, J., Pollard, R., & Taylor, S. (2004). Applications of logistic regression to shots at goal in association football: Calculation of shot probabilities, quantification of factors and player/team. *Journal of Sports Sciences*, 22(6), 500–520.

Fasold, F., Wühr, P., & Memmert, D. (2019). Response requirements affect offside judgments in football (soccer). *Psychological Research*, 83(5), 924–934.

Fontes, P., & Buarque de Hollanda, B. (Eds.). (2014). *The Country of Football: Politics, Popular Culture, and the Beautiful Game in Brazil*. University Press of Florida.

Frigg, R., & Hartmann, S. (n.d.). *Models in Science*. The Stanford Encyclopedia of Philosophy.

Fullerton, T. (2024). *Game Design Workshop: A Playcentric Approach to Creating Innovative Games* (5th ed.). A K Peters/CRC Press.

Gadamer, H.G. (2004). *Truth and Method*. Continuum.

Geppert, L. N., Ickstadt, K., Karl, F., Münch, J., & Steinbrecher, M. (2022). Visualising complex data within a data science loop: A spatio-temporal example from football. In A. Steland & K.-L. Tsui (Eds.), *Artificial Intelligence, Big Data and Data Science in Statistics: Challenges and Solutions in Environmetrics, the Natural Sciences and Technology* (pp. 301–319). Springer International Publishing. https://doi.org/10.1007/978-3-031-07155-3_13

Gigerenzer, G. (2008). *Rationality for Mortals: How People Cope with Uncertainty*. Oxford University Press.

Ginesta, X., de San Eugenio, J., Bonet, P., Ferrer, M. (2020). Global football in the US market. The internationalization of FC Barcelona and its media coverage. *Soccer & Society*, 21(2), 209–224. https://doi.org/10.1080/14660970.2018.1556645

Giulianotti, R. (1999). *Football: A Sociology of the Global Game*. Polity.

Goffman, E. (1961). *Encounters. Two Studies in the Sociology of Interaction*. Bobbs-Merrill.

Goldblatt, D. (2007). *The Ball Is Round: A Global History of Football*. Penguin.

Gumbrecht, H. U. (1999). Epiphany of form: On the beauty of team sports. *New Literary History*, 30(2), 351–372.

Hamil, S., Walters, G., & Watson, L. (2010). The model of governance at FC Barcelona: Balancing member democracy, commercial strategy, corporate social responsibility and sporting performance. *Soccer & Society*, 11(4), 475–504. https://doi.org/10.1080/14660971003780446

Heifetz, A. (2012). *Game Theory*. Cambridge University Press.

Huizinga, J. (1971). *Homo Ludens*. Beacon Press.

Hunter, G. (2012). *Barca: The Making of the Greatest Team in the World*. Backpage Press Limited.

Hüttermann, S., Noël, B., Memmert, D., & Sampaio, J. (2017). Evaluating erroneous offside calls in soccer. *Plos One*, 12(3).

Joseph, D. J. (2018). The Discourse of Digital Dispossession: Paid Modifications and Community Crisis on Steam. *Games and Culture*, 13(7), 690–707.

Joseph, D. (2021). Battle pass capitalism. *Journal of Consumer Culture*, 21(1), 68–83. https://doi.org/10.1177/1469540521993930

Joseph, D., Nieborg, D., & Young, C. J. (2023). One big store: Source diversity and value capture of digital games in national app store instances. *International Journal of Communication*, 17, 7246–7264.

Juul, J. (2002). The open and the closed: Games of emergence and games of progression. *Computer Games and Digital Cultures Conference*, 323–329.

Juul, J. (2005). *Half-Real: Video Games between Real Rules and Fictional Worlds*. MIT Press.

King, A. (2001). *The End of the Terraces: The Transformation of English Football*. Leicester University Press.

Kok, A. (2022). *Johan Cruyff: Always on the Attack*. Simon & Schuster.

Krzyzaniak, J. S. (2018). The soft power strategy of soccer sponsorships. *Soccer & Society*, 19(4), 498–515. https://doi.org/10.1080/14660970.2016.1199426

Link, D. (2018). *Data Analytics in Professional Soccer*. Springer.

Maffesoli, M. (1996). *The Time of the Tribes*. Sage Publications.

Mañas-Viniegra, L. (2018). La aportación internacional de la marca Real Madrid a la ciudad de Madrid (España) como destino turístico de eventos deportivos. *Turismo y Sociedad*, 24, 129–148. https://doi.org/10.18601/01207555.n24.06

Maruenda, F. B. (2004). Can the human eye detect an offside position during a football match? *BMJ* 329, 1470.

Mather, G. (2020). A step to VAR: The vision science of offside calls by video assistant referees. *Perception*, 49(12), 1371–1374.

Mead, J., O'Hare, A., & McMenemy, P. (2023). Expected goals in football: Improving model performance and demonstrating value. *PLOS ONE*, 18(4), e0282295. https://doi.org/10.1371/journal.pone.0282295

Mirkovic, G., Sauer, T., & and Zülch, H. (2025). The game changer in French football: The case of Paris St. Germain. *Soccer & Society*, 26(3), 515–532. https://doi.org/10.1080/14660970.2024.2446970

Montfort, N. and Bogost, I. (2009). *Racing the Beam*. The Atari Video Computer System. The MIT Press.

Nguyen, C. T. (2020). *Games: Agency as Art*. Oxford University Press.

Nieborg, D. B. (2015). Crushing candy: The free-to-play game in its connective commodity form. *Social Media + Society*, 1(2), 2056305115621932. https://doi.org/10.1177/2056305115621932

Nieborg, D. B. (2021). Apps of empire: Global capitalism and the app economy. *Games and Culture*, 16(3), 305–316. https://doi.org/10.1177/1555412020937826

Nieborg, D. B., Duffy, B. E., & Poell, T. (2020). Studying platforms and cultural production: Methods, institutions, and practices. *Social Media + Society*, 6(3), 2056305120943273. https://doi.org/10.1177/2056305120943273

Nieborg, D. B., & Poell, T. (2018). The platformization of cultural production: Theorizing the contingent cultural commodity. *New Media & Society*, 20(11), 4275–4292. https://doi.org/10.1177/1461444818769694

Nieborg, D. B., & Helmond, A. (2019). The political economy of Facebook's platformization in the mobile ecosystem: Facebook Messenger as a platform instance. *Media, Culture & Society*, 41(2), 196–218.

Nieborg, D. B., Young, C. J., & Joseph, D. (2020). *App Imperialism: The Political Economy of the Canadian App Store*. Social Media+Society, 1(2). https://doi.org/10.1177/2056305120933293

Panse, N. & Mahabaleshwarkar, A. (2020). A Dataset & Methodology for Computer Vision based Offside Detection in Soccer. *Proceedings of the 3rd International Workshop on Multimedia Content Analysis in Sports*, 19–26.

Papoulis, A. (1984). *Probability, Random Values and Stochastic Processes*. McGraw-Hill.

Pearson, G. (2012). *An Ethnography of English Football Fans: Cans, Cops and Carnivals*. Manchester University Press.

Perarnau, M. (n.d.). *La evolución táctica del fútbol 1863—1945: Descifrando el código genético del fútbol de la mano del falso 9*. Roca Editorial.

Perarnau, M. (2014a). *Herr Pep: Crónica desde dentro de su primer año en el Bayern de Múnich*. Roca Editorial.

Perarnau, M. (2014b). *Pep Confidential: The Inside Story of Pep Guardiola's First Season at Bayern Munich*. Arena Sport.

Perarnau, M. (2016). *Pep Guardiola: The Evolution*. Arena Sport.

Perarnau, M. (2025). *The Pep Revolution: Inside Guardiola's Manchester City*. Ebury Spotlight.

Pitt, J. (2021). Knowing the Unknowable: Soft Laws and Hard Decisions. *IEEE Technology and Society Magazine*, 40(4), 5–9.

Poulton, E. (2007). 'Fantasy football hooliganism' in popular media. *Media, Culture & Society*, 29(1), 151–164.

Pu, Z., Pan, Y., Wang, S., Liu, B., Chen, M., Ma, H., & Cui, Y. (2024). Orientation and decision-making for soccer based on sports analytics and AI: A systematic review. *IEEE/CAA Journal of Automatica Sinica*, 11(1), 37–57. https://doi.org/10.1109/JAS.2023.123807

Rein, R., & Memmert, D. (2016). Big data and tactical analysis in elite soccer: Future challenges and opportunities for sports science. *SpringerPlus*, 5(1), 1410. https://doi.org/10.1186/s40064-016-3108-2

Rohde, M., & Breuer, C. (2017). The market for football club investors: A review of theory and empirical evidence from professional European football.

European Sport Management Quarterly, 17(3), 265–289. https://doi.org/10.1080/16184742.2017.1279203

Russell, S., & Norvig, P. (2021). *Artificial Intelligence: A Modern Approach* (4th ed.). Pearson.

Salen, K., & Zimmerman, E. (2003). *Rules of Play: Game Design Fundamentals*. MIT Press.

Santos, G. (2015). Upward and downward causation from a relational-horizontal ontological perspective. *Axiomathes*, 25(1), 23–40.

Shannon, L. (2021). *Point of Attack: Johann Cruyff, Sun Tzu & The Art of War in Football*. Independently Published.

Sharp, J. (2015). *Works of Game On the Aesthetics of Games and Art*. The MIT Press.

Sicart, M. (2008). Defining Game Mechanics. *Game Studies* 8(2). https://gamestudies.org/0802/articles/sicart

Sicart, M. (2014). *Play Matters*. MIT Press.

Sicart, M. (2015). Loops and Metagames: Understanding Game Design Structures. *Proceedings of the 10th International Conference on the Foundations of Digital Games (FDG 2015)*, June 22–25, 2015, Pacific Grove, CA, USA.

Sidorenko-Bautista, P., Castillo-Abdul, B., Herranz-de-la-Casa, J-M, & Abellán-Hernández, M. (2025). Marketing, advertising, and branding in Fortnite: How do brands and companies connect today to audiences through the metaverse? *Cogent Social Sciences*, 11(1), 2458058. https://doi.org/10.1080/23311886.2025.2458058

Silver, D., Huang, A., Maddison, C. J., Guez, A., Sifre, L., van den Driessche, G., Schrittwieser, J., Antonoglou, I., Panneershelvam, V., Lanctot, M., Dieleman, S., Grewe, D., Nham, J., Kalchbrenner, N., Sutskever, I., Lillicrap, T., Leach, M., Kavukcuoglu, K., Graepel, T., & Hassabis, D. (2017). Mastering the game of Go with deep neural networks and tree search. *Nature*, 529(7587), 484–489. https://doi.org/10.1038/nature16961

Soto de la Cruz, J., Cortés Gómez, S., & Lacasa, P. (2008). La reinvención del videojuego y nuevas formas de consumo en tiempos de confinamiento. *Caso Fortnite. Comunicación y Sociedad*, 20, 1–23.

Spaaij, R. (2006). *Understanding Football Hooliganism*. AUP.

Steinkuehler, C. A., & Williams, D. (2006). Where everybody knows your (screen) name: Online games as "third places." *Journal of Computer-Mediated Communication*, 11(4), 885–909. https://doi.org/10.1111/j.1083-6101.2006.00300.x

Stenros, J. (2015). *Playfulness, Play, and Games: A Constructionist Ludology Approach*. PhD Thesis, Tampere University Press.

Srnicek, N. (2017). *Platform Capitalism*. Verso Books.

Suits, B. (1978). *The Grasshopper: Games, Life and Utopia*. University of Toronto Press.

Sumpter, D. (2016). *Soccermatics Mathematical Adventures in the Beautiful Game.* Bloomsbury.

Supergiant Games. (2020). *Hades.* Nintendo Switch.

Sutton-Smith, B. (1997). *The Ambiguity of Play.* Harvard University Press.

Svantesson, D. (2014). Could technology resurrect the dignity of the FIFA World Cup refereeing? *Computer Law & Security Review*, 30(5), 569–573.

Tavinor, G. (2009). *The Art of Videogames.* Wiley-Blackwell.

Thornton, P. (2003). *Casuals: Football, Fighting & Fashion: The Story of a Terrace Cult.* Milo Books.

Thorhauge, A.M. (2023a). *Games in the Platform Economy: Steam's Tangled Markets.* Bristol University Press.

Thorhauge, A.M. (2023b). The steam platform economy: From retail to player-driven economies. *New Media & Society*, 26(4), 1963–1983.

Togelius, J. (2019). *Playing Smart : On Games, Intelligence, and Artificial Intelligence.* The MIT Press.

Turing, A. M. (1950). I.—COMPUTING MACHINERY AND INTELLIGENCE. *Mind LIX*, 236: 433–460.

Viñas, C., & Parra, N. (2020). *St. Pauli: Another Football is Possible.* Pluto Press.

Ward, J. (2009, February 2). *The Forgotten Pioneers of Football: Herbert Chapman.* Bleacherreport.Com.

Wein, H. (2007). *Developing Youth Football Players.* Human Kinetics Publishers.

White, J. R. (2024). Multimodal and commercial identity work by Fortnite content creators. *Journal of Gaming & Virtual Worlds,* 16(1), 47–67. Intellect. https://doi.org/10.1386/jgvw_00091_1

Wiener, N. (1961). *Cybernetics.* The MIT Press.

Wilson, J. (2008). *Inverting the Pyramid. The History of Football Tactics.* Orion Books.

Wilson, J. (2016). *Angels with Dirty Faces: How Argentinian Soccer Defined a Nation and Changed the Game Forever.* Orion Books.

Winner, D. (2000). *Brilliant Orange. The Neurotic Genius of Dutch Football.* Bloomsbury.

Wright, W. (n.d.). Sculpting Possibility Space. http://itc.conversationsnetwork.org/shows/detail376.html

Yannakakis, G. N., & Togelius, J. (2018). *Artificial Intelligence and Games.* Springer International Publishing. https://doi.org/10.1007/978-3-319-63519-4

Zuberk. R. (2020). *Elements of Game Design.* The MIT Press.

Zuboff, Shoshana. *In the Age of the Smart Machine: The Future of Work and Power.* Basic Books, 1988.

Index

For Product Safety Concerns and Information please contact our EU representative GPSR@taylorandfrancis.com
Taylor & Francis Verlag GmbH, Kaufingerstraße 24, 80331 München, Germany

www.ingramcontent.com/pod-product-compliance
Ingram Content Group UK Ltd.
Pitfield, Milton Keynes, MK11 3LW, UK
UKHW021515250926
475702UK00043B/645
9781041068037